Scotland's Golf in Days of Steam

First Published 2000 by
SCOTTISH CULTURAL PRESS
Unit 13d, Newbattle Abbey Business Annexe
Newbattle Road
Dalkeith EH22 3LJ
Tel: 0131 660 6366 • Fax: 0131 660 6414
e-mail: info@scottishbooks.com • web: www.scottishbooks.com

BRITISH LIBRARY CATALOGUING IN PUBLICATION DATA
A catalogue record for this book is available from the British Library

ISBN: 1 84017 034 4

Printed and bound by Colour Books Ltd, Dublin

Scotland's Golf
in
Days *of* Steam

A Selective History of the Impact of the Railways on Golf

Ian Nalder

SCOTTISH CULTURAL PRESS

Contents

Foreword

Sir Bob Reid, Deputy Governor of the Bank of Scotland
& Chairman of British Rail 1990–95

I grew up in Fife. When golf became an essential part of my life St Andrews was almost a second home to me. In common with that great man of letters, Bernard Darwin, I had understood it was on the sixteenth green of the Old Course that Joyce Wethered, the pre-eminent lady golfer between the Wars, concentrated so greatly on holing a telling putt she was oblivious to a passing train as it thundered by. Her reply to the question 'Hadn't she been distracted by the train?' is now part of legend. 'What train?' she said.

When asked about this incident later in life, Joyce answered she thought the setting had been Sheringham. Possibly some vestige of doubt remains. After all she never heard the train. No matter! The legend lives on!

A further fascinating train story also related to Joyce, an event that took place at Troon. It is one of countless vignettes unearthed here. Happily this remarkable lady features not a little since she learned her golf at Royal Dornoch. In her eyes this was the finest links of all.

In fact, the story of the railways and golf is rich in its connections and is as much about massive investment in courses and hotels as it is about opening up the country for leisure and pleasure. Above all it was an important chapter in the history of golf – it brought people to the game and a respect for the links which has lasted. Those on the Dundee–Aberdeen Express in 1999 had the best view at Carnoustie when they watched the leader at the last hole of the Open go paddling in the Barry Burn.

Ian in this book captures the history and magic in a way which will not only entertain but may inspire many readers to make the journey and test their skills. By rail that journey can still be more pleasant and certainly less arduous!

Acknowledgements

Had it not been for Dr Melissa Hardie's unexpected request to contribute to the series of Patten People, I doubt this book would ever have come about. In the course of working on *A Glance Along the Tracks*, which involved personal recollections of the railways and golf, it dawned on me there was a more substantial volume waiting to be written. So, Melissa, thank you for planting the seed.

A special word of thanks is due Ian Marchbank and Don Macleod. Ian was for many years the golf professional at Turnberry and then Gleneagles. He helped me to appreciate the strong connection between railways, holidays, hotels and golf. He also provided me with the results of his own research into the early days of Gleneagles. Don, a boy caddie at Brora who later retired there, was a fund of information on both the north of Scotland and Joyce Wethered.

Thanks, too, to Gordon Huddy for alerting me to Nisbet's *Golf Year Book* of 1914, to Sir Robert Speed for his recollections of university golf, to David Hamilton, Laurie Ing and John McConachie for their encouragement, and to the many club secretaries who have freely assisted – almost all those asked! My gratitude also to Michael Attenborough for his advice; to Archie Baird, Bill Dryden, James Hardie and Alan Mickel for the loan or gift of fascinating club histories; to David St John Thomas for his time and kindness in joining me in foraging through his archives of railway photographs; to John Wolstenholme for the 1857 *Rules of Golf*; and to the General Manager of the Turnberry Hotel for a copy of the *Illustrated History of British Railway Hotels*.

Last, but by no means least, I have greatly appreciated the efficient services of the London Library, the Mitchell Library in Glasgow, the National Railway Museum and the Scottish Records Office.

SCOTLAND

ORKNEY ISLANDS

SHETLAND ISLANDS

Brora
Golspie
Royal
Dornoch
Hopeman
Moray
Tain
Strathlene
Strathpeffer
Spa
Forres
Spey Bay
Cullen
Nairn
Elgin
Cruden Bay
Grantown
Boat of Garten
Newtonmore
Kingussie
Panmure
St Andrews
Gleneagles
Gullane
Glasgow
Gailes
North Berwick
Western Gailes
Machrihanish
Prestwick
Turnberry
Silloth

0   50mls

Map of Featured Golf Courses

12

List of Featured Golf Courses

Boat of Garten
Brora
Cruden Bay
Cullen
Elgin
Forres
Glasgow Gailes
Gleneagles
Golspie
Grantown
Gullane
Hopeman
Kingussie
Machrihanish
Moray

Nairn
Newtonmore
North Berwick
Panmure
Prestwick
Royal Dornoch
St Andrews
Silloth
Spey Bay
Strathlene
Strathpeffer Spa
Tain
Turnberry
Western Gailes

Also mentioned are:

Barassie, Carnoustie, Garmouth & Kingston, Irvine, Killermont, Machrie, Monifieth, Montrose, Muirfield, Musselburgh, Nairn Dunbar, Royal Troon, Sheringham, Shiskine, Skibo.

Introduction

The heyday of Britain's railways coincided with an extraordinary growth in the popularity of golf. In some cases railway companies actively assisted this, going so far as to construct a station alongside the course and sometimes even building the line to get there. In rare instances they actually commissioned the golf course. One railway company even provided the members with a clubhouse. Expecting good revenue along the adjoining line, they accepted a rental of only £7 a year. More commonplace was the keenest competition between the various railway companies to build grand hotels for golfers. Each aimed at providing a holiday paradise with golf as the principal pastime.

Up until the 1920s golf was conceived as good for their business. Nowadays, however, the railways have only the slightest impact upon the golfer. Many of the lines which once were a feature of the course, and a source of terror to the player, have long disappeared; in their place a walkway or gardens somehow act as less of a magnet.

The current golfing renaissance mirrors the activity of a century ago, but today's stars are names known across and beyond the golfing world. Media interest in all aspects of the professional game is intense. Even those with little or no interest will know the names of Nick Faldo, Seve Ballesteros and Tiger Woods. This has happened quite apart from any radical rebirth in the railways if, indeed, this is what privatisation of the rail network will produce.

What follows is a look at the legacy left to golf by the railways; a story formed through social history and anecdote. Bernard Darwin is the source of certain inspiration, for in his day he was a golf writer without equal, possessed with a special affection for both the game and the railways. He was a fine player, good enough to perform for his country, and he wrote simple but beautiful English. From 1907 he contributed regularly to *Country Life* for over half a century and for many years was also the golf correspondent for *The Times*, though in the fashion of the day his authorship remained incognito.

As for the golf courses, described more in spirit than in detail, it is the joy and challenge that come across. Selecting these has been an unenviable task. Why, you may ask, when near neighbours feature, is there no record of Royal Troon or Carnoustie, both of which are venues for the Open? And what about Royal Aberdeen — a mesmerising course if ever there was one, but so popular among the local people not to need its own railway.

Should I be pardoned for these omissions, I hope that the tales surrounding those that do feature will entertain and, moreover, that the inclusion of a little slice of Scotland in England, namely Silloth, will be welcomed. If as a result you are tempted to see for yourself, to play the links that are the subject of affectionate comment, to absorb the atmosphere, and to marvel at the silver trophies and artefacts displayed, my hope is that your leisure will be enriched. There is remarkable heritage here waiting to be explored.

Rise and Fall

In his old age the Duke of Wellington had grown downright crusty. Here was an Irish aristocrat, a general and a politician, who had masterminded many successful campaigns in Spain before beating Napoleon in 1815 at Waterloo, now preferring to live out life in seclusion at Stratfield Saye. Rather curiously, as a former leader of men and Prime Minister, he was not to welcome the coming of the railways. He saw them as a threat to the status quo – to a domestic stability in which people knew their place for the railways offered the masses the opportunity to move around.

Wellington was right of course. The railways did just that. All sorts and classes of people were happy to use the train, and railway entrepreneurs went to no end of trouble to encourage them either through tailored prices or the provision of unashamed luxury.

Within two decades the Duke had passed on and the railways had overcome misgivings such as his. Instead they were winning an affectionate place in the hearts of the nation, if for no better reason than they made possible holidays by the sea. Although the industrial revolution was not far advanced, many had little option other than to seek their living in a city. For them one week at the seaside became a very real goal, a treat for the family and something worth saving for. So it was that coastal resorts sprung up and fishing villages saw a proliferation of hotels, boarding houses, even *pieds-a-terre*. Railway companies sung their praises willingly enough. They knew if they encouraged day-dreams, demand for their services would increase, and as resorts developed a virtuous cycle would be created. This expansion of the holiday market was to become very big business for them.

The growth of Brighton in the south of England illustrates the point. In the ten years prior to 1851 the population soared by 20,000. Eight years later, 73,000 visitors were to arrive by train in just one week. Departing Waterloo every half-hour, they must have been packed to the 'gunnels'.

With the seaside becoming such a draw, there was the keenest competition between railway companies to win custom. The most favoured medium for this was poster advertising and town councils contributed gladly to the cost. All over Britain station posters would proclaim the appeal of distant holiday spots, the most famous being the roistering fisherman alongside the slogan 'Skegness is so bracing'. Leading graphic artists were commissioned, even Royal Academicians such as Augustus John, and today the best examples of poster art are highly valued.

After the Great War when golf began to be fashionable among the middle classes and provided a good reason for a holiday, golf links were to feature on posters. The London Midland & Scottish Railway promoted the Northern Ireland resorts of Portrush and Newcastle, County Down; the Great Western went after the long-distance traveller to southern Ireland via the Fishguard to Rosslare ferry service; and the London North East Railway at first promoted golf in East Anglia and the better inland courses like Woodhall Spa before extolling Northumberland as the Golfer's Elysium and, later, encouraging even longer distance travel to Scotland. Not to be undone, the Southern Railway sported golfing posters for Bournemouth and Seaford, produced a free booklet under the title *Golfing in Southern England and on the Continent* and a book called *Some Friendly Fairways*. The book provides a humorous glimpse into early golfing life. One anecdote concerns a 70-year-old caddie. A long-serving lifeboatman, daring and forthright, he was reported as upbraiding his player:

Skegness is so bracing: 1926 version of the famous Great Northern Railway poster of 1908 *(courtesy of the National Railway Museum/Science & Society Picture Library)*

'Scotland for Holidays' – 'Deer Stalking in the Highlands' by W. Smithson Broadhead
(courtesy of the National Railway Museum/Science & Society Picture Library)

You shouldn't 'ave given 'em all these bisques, Sir, 'tain't right; but we'll do 'em in yet. Take the spoon and play on that there bush – see? That's the shot. We've got this 'ole in our pockets.

Could the *double-entendre* have been intended?

Another story is told of a gentleman whose skills cannot match his enthusiasm. He is yet to get round in 90, through he has promised his regular caddie that when this happens he will benefit by £50. One day both he and the caddie are agog, for he has arrived on the last green in 88 shots. The goal is in sight. Imagine the mounting tension. The caddie's mind is firmly fixed on how the windfall is going to be spent that night but, alas, the gentleman's excitement overcomes him and the green requires not two but five putts! The caddie looks glum and the player is visibly crestfallen. Next time they meet the inevitable awkwardness is quickly dissolved as the caddie is handed a silver watch suitably inscribed!

For all this rival publicity, it was Scotland, in the wake of Queen Victoria and her love of the Highlands, which was to win the battle to become the playground for the well-to-do. The constant allure of fishing, shooting and stalking combined with golf to provide the perfect retreat. The railways led the way and where hotels were required the railway companies vied among themselves to outdo each other. At one time there were 113 railway hotels in England, Scotland and Wales with a further 31 in Ireland. Most have now been demolished or converted into flats, homes or offices, and the rest are in private ownership. Each hotel was a world apart from the simple, traditional Railway Inn or Station Hotel that were principally local enterprise stopovers for passengers requiring a bed for the night, or hostels to accommodate supervisors as the line was being built.

Of the few spectacular former railway hotels that remain and are now enjoying better days, two – Gleneagles and Turnberry – were built solely on account of golf. Now the railway is relevant no more to the hotels it spawned.

It is a fair question how much golf and the railways ever had in common.

Golfers on holiday: returning from a day out in Oban
(*courtesy of Locomotive & General Railways Photographs*)

The answer is rather more than one might have supposed. Until the Great War the tendency was for golf to follow where steam led; then, between the wars, development around courses mushroomed, making it easier for players to use their cars. In the 1950s the relationship was gradually disintegrating and by 1960 the popularity of the motorcar was set on an eight-fold expansion over thirty years. Then came Dr Beeching, Chairman of British Rail, with an axe which he wielded with the connivance and blessing of a grateful government convinced the railways had long seen their heyday. Rural lines were the main casualties. Where the golfer has access to a train now, that is fortuitous, though the chances are it will be in Scotland, the home of golf.

St Andrews – the Home of Golf

The relationship between St Andrews and golf is even stronger than that between Newmarket and horse-racing or between Lords and cricket. Very simply, St Andrews is a place of pilgrimage where virtually every golfer of repute throughout the world wills to play at least once in a lifetime. It is not just that this old university town is charm personified or that the links touches its very heart. St Andrews is more than that. It is both the home of golf and its legislative body, and as such plays a dynamic role.

Since 1123, when King David I granted it to the bishops, the course has been the property of the ancient city of St Andrews. Successive charters have been careful to ensure that the citizens' rights to the links have been maintained. It is not clear when golf was first played there but certainly by 1413, when the university was founded, it was already popular. Not that everyone was in favour of the pastime. In fact in 1457 King James II sought to ban it and the Scottish Parliament decreed 'that Fute-ball and Golfe be utterly cryit down and nocht usit'.

This antipathy 'anent gowffing' existed because it was considered 'an unprofitable sport for the common good of the realm and the defence thereof'. It was claimed that golf distracted the Scots from archery and to counter its attraction, sheriffs were charged with setting up butts, skill with the bow and arrow was encouraged, and golf was forbidden; anyone caught playing it was likely to be fined. Antagonism towards the game had also been inflamed because a man in Brechin had been murdered with a golf club.

If the King thought he could stamp out golf, he was mistaken. In 1552 Archbishop Hamilton of St Andrews spelt out the citizens' rights. The links were there to be enjoyed for golf, football, shooting and, indeed, 'all other maner of pastyme as ever thei pleis'. The links was under the control of the church; they approved and that was that. However, another two centuries were to pass before the game became organised.

The forerunner of the Royal & Ancient Golf Club was the Society of St

Andrews Golfers. Founded in 1754 by 22 distinguished men from the Kingdom of Fife, all were avid golfers and each was concerned with keeping in check a practice which was inimical to their pleasure. The threat was real for at the time the Town Council were in the habit of granting leaseholds over portions of the links for the purpose of . . . breeding rabbits!

In terms of seniority the Society was bettered by the Gentlemen Golfers at Leith. They had formed their association ten years earlier even though, just as at St Andrews, golf had been played there informally over many previous years. Indeed King Charles I was said to have been at Leith links in 1641 at the time he was informed the Irish were in revolt. When the Gentlemen considered that play over five holes was too restrictive, they moved to a nine-hole layout at Musselburgh. Ultimately, they settled at Muirfield and changed their name to the Honourable Company of Edinburgh Golfers.

In 1754 the Society followed the Gentlemen's example and commissioned a

Poster promoting the LNER illustrated free booklet *(courtesy of the National Railway Museum/Science & Society Picture Library)*

silver club as a trophy. This was engraved with a portrait of St Andrew. The winner became 'Captain of the Golf' and the practice continued through until 1824. Like the Leith men, they drew up some rules for play. There numbered just 13 but they were sufficiently thoughtful for other clubs to turn to the Society for advice. So were born the rules of golf.

In those early days play at St Andrews was over 22 holes. The format was 11 holes out followed by the same holes played in reverse order home again. This explains the remarkable feature of so many vast double greens. In 1834 King William IV agreed to be the Society's patron and conferred upon it the title of the 'Royal & Ancient Golf Club of St Andrews'. Change soon followed and two years later the course was reduced to nine holes out and nine holes back. Somehow it was felt this was the ideal number, although it took a while for the concept of 18 holes to become accepted wisdom. Montrose retained its 25 holes and even now on the Isle of Arran play is over 12 holes at Blackwaterfoot's Shiskine course.

Within ten years separate teeing grounds were introduced. The original practice of teeing off within two club lengths of the hole just played was seen not only as harmful to the green but possibly rather dangerous. They also called a halt to the habit of taking sand from the bottom of the hole in order to tee up the shot to the next one since the holes were getting so deep it was becoming difficult to extricate the ball. Sand was still used to tee the ball up but this was provided in nearby boxes.

For twenty years the Royal & Ancient shared the cosy parlour premises of the St Andrews Union Club. Then in 1855 the two amalgamated. That was the occasion to build the present magnificent clubhouse. Now there was visible evidence that St Andrews was the *alma mater* of golf.

In 1852 the railway reached the ancient city. Among the active local promoters was Robert Haig of the John Haig whisky family. The short branch line joined the Edinburgh, Perth and Dundee railway at Leuchars, but the junction was not an instant success for it was reported, 'the directors are aware of the great detention of passengers . . . and are endeavouring to make arrangements to have this great annoyance removed'.

Worse still for the prosperity of the branch was the legacy of its engineer Thomas Bouch. Strapped for cash, he built the line on the cheap and it was therefore little more than a light railway. The sleepers were spaced at four feet instead of the usual three feet, and the rails were fastened to them with treenails – wooden pins – rather than metal spikes. The result was that the Edinburgh, Perth and Dundee locomotive was too heavy to run on the branch line.

Yet the little railway to St Andrews survived more than a century. In so doing it happened to play an important part in the golf course, for it formed the boundary to the right of the fourteenth, fifteenth and sixteenth holes before being even more provocative at the seventeenth. This was due to the need to avoid a triangle of land that juts out, but over which the brave player's well-stuck drive obtains a substantial advantage. This plot which continues to threaten has been home to many and varied activities: hickory laid out to dry, the station master's garden, coal sheds, and now, in place of the names of the one-time coal merchants, is painted 'Old Course Hotel, Golf Resort & Spa'. Today it is no less daunting as the tiger line, which lies over the word 'Hotel', is still no soft option. The hotel itself, offspring of the old British Railway, is now run by a hugely successful international company for the delight of multi-millionaire champions and golfing pilgrims the world over.

Initially, the railway line had not been out of bounds and was treated as an integral part of the course. A decision as to what should happen if a ball were to finish on the tracks was not long in coming; under the Royal & Ancient Rules of May 1857 it was stated:

XX   Ball on Railway – Should a ball betwixt the rails, the player shall have the option of playing it, or lifting it and dropping it behind him, losing a stroke (See Rule VII)

VII   In all cases where the ball is to be dropped, the party doing so shall front the hole to which he is playing, standing close on the hazard, and drop the ball behind him from his head.

These were the rules governing the Open in 1905 when James Braid was on the way to his second Open victory. This account of the final round is in Braid's own words and comes from his book *Advanced Golf.* It may well provide the sensitive with a chill feeling in the pit of the stomach as it relates to the most awesome drama on the tracks ever to involve a champion.

Then came the railway . . . Going to the fifteenth I sliced my second shot on to it. Playing off it I hit a man and the ball rebounded from him and went to a nasty place, where it was tucked up against a bush. The hole cost me six . . .

But at the next hole . . . I drove right over the Principal's Nose and pitched into the bunker beyond . . . I became too venturesome and attempted to put the ball on to the green . . . instead . . . I got it on the railway (again!) and when I went up to it I found it lying in a horrible place, being tucked up against iron chairs in which the rails rest. It was on the left-hand side of the right-hand rail, playing towards the hole, and the only crumb of comfort was that it was not on the other side of either of the rails.

I took my niblick and tried to hook it out but did not succeed, the ball moving only a few yards, and being in much the same position against the rail.

With my fourth, however, I got it back on the course, but in a very difficult position.

It went some 30 yards past the hole near to the bunker on the left of the second green . . . I had only about a yard to come and go on with a run-up shot, which was plainly the proper stroke to play in the circumstances, if I wanted to get close to the hole as I must do if I was to get a 6. It was . . . bold and very risky . . . but . . . it came off, the ball running dead.

In all the four rounds of that Championship I think it was the best shot that I played . . . I was excusably very anxious, and knew that everything depended on it . . . It put new heart into me, and I tackled the seventeenth without any fear . . . and I won with five strokes to spare.

Braid's talents as a golf-course designer were particularly in demand in Scotland. With tournaments and exhibition matches being held in England in the main, he used the trains a lot. Putting the experience of that championship behind him, Braid was a big enough man in every sense not to dissent from the view that, regardless of comfort, the railway was a wonderful way to end the pilgrimage to St Andrews, especially when travelling over the mile-long, 157-foot-high bridge spanning the Eden south of Leuchars.

In 1966 Henry Longhurst, former captain, essayist, raconteur and commentator *extraordinaire*, headlined one of his regular articles for *The Sunday Times*: 'You Can't Let Them Do It, Barbara'. The lady in question was none other than the Labour Minister of Transport, Barbara Castle. Longhurst had just learned of the proposal, which he described as being made 'quietly, almost furtively, and in very small print', to abandon the railway and close the station. A lover of the sleeper from London to Scotland where, in his words, one would wake up 'in a new world of hillsides, burns, a dashing river and air like champagne', he considered this journey could only be surpassed by the little two-coach to 'St Andra's' – for this was the cry that echoed along the exposed platform at Leuchars – as the most memorable train journey in the world. Not that diesel technology fascinated him. His thoughts harked back to the veteran steam engine which rejoiced in the name Kettledrummle, and how it would happily take one:

Round the corner to Guard Bridge, past that fellow's immaculate vegetable garden and the papermill, across the bridge over the Eden – the driver having already twice leaned out to exchange those big rings with leather pouches attached in order to secure his right of way – and alongside the estuary with, at low tide, its innumerable birds on the mudflats. In the distance now the singular, unforgettable outline of the 'Old Grey Town' with its spires and towers and the ruins of the cathedral . . .

Passing the black sheds over which you drive at the Road Hole, we see the Little Road Bunker, in which every guest golfer has at sometime stood, with the same thoughts running through his head, and behind the green the dreaded road itself.

A quick glimpse of the Royal & Ancient clubhouse standing foursquare behind the first tee and we are rounding the bend with a cheerful toot to announce our arrival at the little station, where dedicated hands have traced out on the bank in white stones the legend: *St Andrews. Home of Golf.* The golfer is home indeed.

His words went unheeded and the line was one more casualty of Beeching's remit.

It must be admitted that others, including Sam Snead, were not such devotees of the line. In any count of the world's greatest players, this supreme American stylist is sure to feature. He took part in the 1937 Open at Carnoustie. In contrast to the manicured courses of his home country this offered a singularly tough challenge on a public course in rough conditions. It was here that Henry Cotton scored his second victory with a brilliant final round in drenching rain. Snead had been as steady as a rock and finished in the first six. He was ten shots behind Cotton but enjoyed neither the town of Carnoustie nor its inhospitable weather.

So it was primarily to seek a place in the history books and to raise the fee he commanded for personal appearances, that his sponsor, the Wilson Sports Goods Company, persuaded Snead to enter for the first post-war Open. America's leading golfer between the wars, Walter Hagen, had helped him with his putting, advising him to strike the ball above the equator. On seeing the immediate improvement in Snead, Hagen urged him to go over to St Andrews and win. Playing at the home of golf meant considerably less to Snead than the thought of how many dollars he might be foregoing by his absence from the American tour that followed the sun.

The railway journey from London did little to reassure him. Throughout the war the country's railways were starved of investment and it is hardly any wonder that Snead described the train from Euston as a 'gully-jumper'. His recall of the scene on finally approaching St Andrews is picturesque, if hardly tactful: 'so raggedy and beat up, I was surprised to see what looked like a fairway amongst the weeds. Down home we would not plant cow beets on land like that'.

Be that as it may, he remembered arriving in St Andrews with his hand on his heart and praying this would not prove to be the place of pilgrimage to which he had travelled several thousand miles. Somewhat guilelessly, Snead tapped the knee of an erstwhile and silent senior citizen sitting across the aisle and asked the name of the 'old abandoned golf course'. In an instant, furore replaced the frigid silence. Snead was lambasted with the full title of the Royal & Ancient, the year it was founded, and with a snort the firm intimation 'it is not now, nor ever will be, abandoned'. The impression left was unforgettable: this was holy ground second only to Westminster Abbey!

If Snead had got off to an inauspicious start, worse was to follow. In the first four days he was to use four different caddies. One whistled between his teeth when Snead was putting – never the strongest part of his game in any case. One could not judge distance to save his life, and one finished up in jail on a charge of drunkenness the night before the first round of the championship proper. The latter was alleged to be St Andrews' best caddie and certainly he was some character. He got himself sprung and begged Snead for the winning ball after his victory by four shots over Bobby Locke and fellow American Johnny Bulla. Snead placed little monetary value on the ball and in that moment of glory succumbed to the entreaties of the hero-worshipping caddie and his promise to treasure it all his days. One hour later the ball, so artfully won, changed hands in a back street bar for £50. In fact, the caddie made more out of the Open than Snead himself after the £150 first prize had been whittled away by expenses.

The 'Old Course', St Andrews, with the Royal & Ancient clubhouse in the background *(photograph by Bill Roberton)*

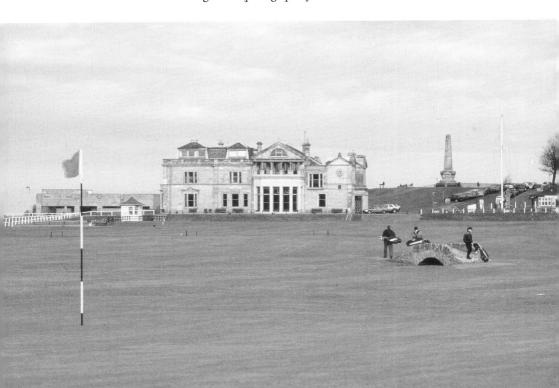

Snead's winning score was 290 – a remarkable effort considering the ferocious wind. So virulent was it that the Belgian maestro Flory van Donck chose to improvise on one green by putting away from the hole, up a slope, in the hope of seeing the ball trickle back closer to the hole – which it did!

Perhaps it is the obligation to learn the art of finesse that holds the player in thrall to St Andrews' secret. It continues to be the scene of many Open Championships and, while it may no longer be as fearsome as it was in Braid's day when the tracks were in play, it remains unique. It demands mastery of every type of shot. At the home of golf who would have it any other way?

Prestwick and the Gallant American

Prestwick has gained a coveted niche in the annals of the game which is in part due to the fact that in 1860 a tournament was held there to ascertain who was the finest player around. The previous year, Allan Robertson of St Andrews, the man long acknowledged as the best, had died. Under the guiding hand of the Earl of Eglinton eight professionals were invited. The contest was over three rounds of 12 holes and the winner was Willie Park of Musselburgh, known to history as Willie Park Snr. At a cost of £25 the club had commissioned a red leather Challenge Belt complete with handsome silver decorations as the trophy. Money was not on offer but anyone who won the coveted belt for three successive years was entitled to keep it.

The following year, when amateurs were admitted, the Open became truly open and the winner was Old Tom Morris. Despite the fact that he was keeper of the green at Prestwick for 14 years, Old Tom was a resolute St Andrews man. Every year apart from one, he and Willie Park vied with each other for the championship, until 1867, when it became the turn of his son, Young Tom Morris. He won it three times in a row and so retained the belt. The authorities were seemingly unprepared for this young man, who would take on the best ball of three opponents and still win, and with no trophy now to play for, the 1871 Open was not held. One can imagine the red faces and recriminations.

In 1872 an agreement between Scotland's three premier clubs – Prestwick, the Royal & Ancient of St Andrews, and the Honourable Company of Edinburgh Golfers (then located at Musselburgh) – meant that a silver claret jug was subscribed. Each course in turn was to be played recommencing at Prestwick. Once again the winner was Young Tom Morris. His cash prize was £8.

At that time challenge matches were a regular feature. In September 1875, both Toms, Old and Young, journeyed from St Andrews to North Berwick to take on Willie Park and his brother Mungo. Willie was the current Open Champion and Mungo had won the previous year. In this challenge the Morrises won on the last green, but their joy was short-lived. Young Tom was

Old Tom Morris in later life

handed a telegram; his wife, who was expecting their child, was seriously ill. With no train readily available, they accepted the offer of a return by yacht across the Firth of Forth and around by Crail. A second message arrived as they were boarding. This reported the deaths of both mother and child. Old Tom held his counsel and did not break the news until they were walking up from the harbour. It devastated his talented son. He lost all interest in life and his livelihood – golf – and it was with reluctance that he played one more challenge medal match, winning by 9/7 against an eccentric character known as Old Mole from Royal North Devon. Retreating into himself, Young Tom was found dead in bed on Christmas Day, broken-hearted. He had been the idol of Scotland at age 24.

It is Prestwick's long association with the Open that arguably makes it the most historic course in Scotland after St Andrews. True to the general form, the railway preceded the golf course, for it was in 1849 that the Glasgow & South Western Railway built the line to Ayr, so opening up the west coast. The clubhouse at Prestwick was built immediately next to the station. The land for both belonged to the Earl of Eglinton, who sensibly negotiated the right to stop trains at whim either by communicating with the guard or station master. A gate provided access to and from the club's precincts, and a warning bell would sound in the clubhouse when a train for Glasgow was approaching. In due course special return tickets for golfers were issued from Glasgow St Enoch at a cost of five shillings. Ordinary passengers who were not golfers obtained no such concession.

Willie Park Snr. was a four-time winner of the Open. Willie Jnr. was nearly as meritorious and shares with Young Tom Morris the distinction of being the only other son to follow in the footsteps of his father and win the Open. First he won in Queen Victoria's Golden Jubilee year (1887) and again two years later. That was fortuitous. He beat Andrew Kirkaldy in a play-off that occurred only due to carelessness by his opponent in the second round. On the fourteenth green, attempting to putt on the lip of the hole one-handed, Kirkaldy had an air shot. A rough and ready wit, he declared, 'If the hole was big enough, I'd bury myself in it'. So he lost his chance of ever becoming Open Champion.

Park might well have won for the third time in 1898 had he understood what was required. The tragedy was he did not. Harry Vardon, the 28 year old from the Channel Island of Jersey, had finished with a pitch and a putt for a birdie 3. Willie was playing immediately behind. He now needed a 3 to tie and popped his second on the green barely a yard away. But between the ball and the hole lay a nasty, hard yarrow weed rather like a carrot top. With no scoreboard, and information limited to word of mouth, Park believed a 4 would earn a tie. Reckoning his only chance of holing the putt was to aim for the back of the hole and skim the ball over the weed with the putter laid back, he dismissed this as a risk not worth taking. So he confided to his caddie, 'I will make sure of the tie and we will have a fine match the morn.' Then, having dribbled the ball to the edge and knocked it in for his 4, he was mortified to learn Vardon had beaten him by one shot. Never again was he to have another opportunity to win.

The Open was held at Prestwick 24 times, the last occasion being the ill-fated event of 1925. This was so dramatic that the anguish and misgivings to which it gave rise resulted in Prestwick being dropped forevermore from the Open roster. The defending champion, Walter Hagen, was absent. He had won at Sandwich in 1922 and then at Hoylake two years later. There a cool head and the Hagen panache had seen him get the better of Ernest Whitcombe, though he had only just escaped being debarred.

The story of this Hoylake battle is curious. The second qualifying round had been at Formby. Hagen and Jim Barnes were staying in Liverpool and together they took the train to Freshfield, only a moment or two away from the club. When they signed in ten minutes behind time they had to argue their case before the committee. Hagen was adamant he had a legitimate excuse. The train was late! He was permitted to play but for some reason Barnes was counted out.

In any case, Hagen was soon in more trouble; on his first round he ran up 83. At Formby's fourth hole he now faced a blind pitch. Waiting patiently for the bell to announce the all-clear, he then holed it. Completing in 73 he scraped in solely on account of that unlikely eagle.

Victory at Hoylake had been sweet but in 1925 Hagen chose not to appear for the Prestwick tournament. Still smarting from that late train a year earlier and his relegation to the sidelines in the Open at Hoylake, it was the Cornish-born and naturalised American, Jim Barnes, who was the leader after the first round. Tall and strong, he belted the ball low, and in-between shots he shambled around looking like a country boy and chewing daisies. As for his golf – 'better than perfect' wrote Bernard Darwin in *The Times*, adding that for once the rumour reverberating around the course did not lie: Barnes was playing like a machine. 'It would be impossible to imagine anything better – very long straight driving, crisp iron play and bold clean putting'.

Requiring 4 3 4 3 for a 69, it was over these last four holes where his coolness proved its worth. The fifteenth green owns as steep a gradient as any that can

The Golfers' Train leaving St Enoch *(courtesy of the Western Gailes Golf Club)*

be found. Here Barnes was interrupted by the capering of an innocent puppy, which gave the impression of never having met anyone quite so nice as Mr Barnes, or seen a ball so succulent for chewing. It took a score of perspiring policemen, and several irritable stewards swearing and running around, before the matter was under control. Barnes duly got his 4 and followed with an easy 3 at Cardinal's Back where he nearly drove the green.

It was at the seventeenth when disaster appeared to strike. Barnes under-clubbed on the blind second to find a hideous hanging lie in the rough grass on the verge of the sand. 'Amid a cumulative deathliness of silence' (to quote Darwin's elegant phraseology), he adopted several stances before managing a very fine shot. This skidded up the bank the far side. Though a good chip and a putt of eight foot meant a 5, it afforded welcome relief. A 3 now would give him a 70. With a glorious shot he drove the last green and the putt shivered over the hole for a 2. So 70 it was.

However, more than Barnes, the man who captured the imagination of the game's addicts was Macdonald Smith, a most elegant stylist. In search of fame and fortune, he, too, had adopted American nationality but, as a former native of Carnoustie, the Scots considered him one of their own, especially as in the previous September he had given a virtuoso display at Gleneagles. Then Aberdonian George Duncan and he had swopped birdies before he ran out the winner in a flurry of brilliance, seven under fours on the second day. Here at Prestwick two sixes had spoiled his morning round, but in the afternoon he stormed in with a record 69 to lead the field by two shots. It was a gallant and gracious performance.

The next morning it seemed that every golfer in the west of Scotland was aiming to get to the Open; and once more the railways played an integral part in the sport. The Glasgow & South Western Railway worked marvels to convey these hordes. By requisitioning all the available rolling stock, 15,000 excited fans – some say 20,000 – were enabled to descend on Prestwick and incredible scenes followed. Many overpowered the ticket collectors, vaulted the wall on to the course then ran through the bunkers in wild abandon, all in the cause of supporting their Carnoustie-born transatlantic hero.

Macdonald Smith, when aged just 20, had tied the U.S. Open with his brother Alex, and John McDermott. Alex won the play-off. Then for the next two years McDermott carried off the trophy. That was 15 years earlier. Now here he was at the Open, rising 36, without a major title to his credit but acknowledged as a superb striker of the ball, and blessed with flair as well as a glorious rhythmic and flowing swing. He had been third at Troon to Arthur Havers two years earlier, and fourth at Hoylake in 1924 to Walter Hagen. This was to be his chance!

On that second morning he was out in a steady 36, but a 6 at the twelfth, and another at the drive-and-pitch fifteenth spoiled the inward half. Still, his 76 was good enough to put him now five shots ahead of the lanky Barnes and Archie Compston, a great favourite of the Prince of Wales.

In the final round, for the fourth time, he started with par figures 4 3. People were still arriving by train to watch and they only had eyes for Smith. The crowd bustled and jostled and hemmed him in. Play was delayed for minutes at each hole. His concentration suffered and he even doubted the gallery was willing him to win. Three from the edge of the third and fifth meant shots dropped. Visits to bunkers at the seventh and eighth produced a pair of sixes.

Out in 42 he was losing rhythm and confidence, and was prevented from seeing how his long shots finished. He collapsed under the pressure as his normally deft game disintegrated. He took a sad five at the short eleventh, a fiendishly tricky hole in even the slightest of cross breezes, and despite a masterly birdie at the seventeenth, known as the Alps and perhaps the world's most spectacular blind hole, he finished with a regulation par for a horrific 82. A distraught Macdonald Smith had tumbled to fourth place, three shots behind, while Compston and pipe-smoking Ted Ray, champion in 1912 and who had improved with each round and ended with a 73, were equal second just one shot behind the winner. Barnes won – rich consolation for being deprived of participation in 1924. The win was impressive and due reward for finishing with seven consecutive fours for a 74. His four-round total was 300.

Had the turbulent crowd really been urging him to win, or possibly harassing him because he had become an American? This was the question that would haunt Smith. Bernard Darwin doubted if he would ever get over the debacle. To him the crowd had been more than human flesh and blood could stand: it had crushed and killed its own favourite. In his coverage of the event, he publicly doubted whether the Open should ever return to Prestwick as the acreage was obviously inadequate to stage-manage the crowds. In fact, it never has done.

Invariably, it is the victor who remains impaled in the memory, but of all the people who have to fill the lesser role, it is perhaps Macdonald Smith who is most deserving of tribute. A complex character, he was said to practise only the shots he played best, cultivating good habits rather than correcting bad ones. In 1934 at Royal St George's, Sandwich, when the field was pulverised by Henry Cotton's scorching first three rounds of 66, 65 and 67, Smith was heard to say he was going out to practise holing brassie shots! In this wry sense of humour one detects his sense of fate. Still a class player, he came fourth.

Maybe Smith was unlucky in the age in which he lived. He was at his peak during the era of fellow Americans Walter Hagen and Bobby Jones, and to appreciate the dominance of these two one need only comment that between them, from 1922 to 1930, they won the Open seven times.

Yet Macdonald Smith came close. After that crucial loss of confidence at Prestwick, and staying away for three years, he was twice runner-up. In 1930 at Hoylake he came second to Bobby Jones, who beat him by just two shots. Then, at Princes, Sandwich, in 1932 with a 70, Smith made up four shots in the final round. But Gene Sarazen, the New York son of an immigrant Italian cabinetmaker, had spread-eagled the field and was home and dry five shots ahead.

However, it was in 1931 at Carnoustie when he was rising 42 that his best opportunity had come. Smith was back in the town of his childhood and longing to get his hands on the famous claret jug. His third round was inspirational. With a 71 he made up six shots on fellow Scot and naturalised American, Tommy Armour. Bernard Darwin explained the climax of the final round:

> He wanted 3, 4, 5 par golf, to beat Armour, and could afford to lose one stroke and yet tie with him. He lost four strokes in two holes and finished 5, 6, 5. I saw the six at the seventeenth, without his ball touching any form of hazard, and I felt rather as if I had gone to see a man hanged.

Macdonald Smith at the fourteenth tee, Prestwick, 1925 Open
(courtesy of Prestwick Golf Club)

Darwin had not witnessed the tee shot at the sixteenth trickle into a bunker. The recovery was good but from eight yards Smith foozled. Nerves were getting the better of him and he missed the next to take three putts. At the seventeenth, his adrenaline pumping, Smith's second shot was simply too good. It flew the flag but settled in thick grass on a hanging lie 20 yards beyond. It was miserable luck – and sixty years before the invention of the lob wedge! Fearful of a squeezed blow and a scuttle to the other side, he botched his chip, and with that his title hope were blown. He was not even runner-up.

Despite this, Smith never forgot his attachment to Scotland, and neither did his wife. On his death, she bequeathed his medals and trophies to his old golf club at Carnoustie. Henry Cotton made the formal presentation and a photograph from his golfing album shows a total of 27.

Were Macdonald Smith to revisit Prestwick today he would find little has changed. Tradition reigns and larger-than-life characters revel in the camaraderie, the after lunch kümmel, and the ensuing challenge on the links. Old-fashioned it may be, but for any lover of the game's history a visit has to be *the* most pressing priority. Here is golf on a grand scale at its most natural. The mind can only boggle how it must have been when play was with hickory-shafted clubs and a gutty ball. The ordeal suffered by Macdonald Smith, that gallant American, will continue to haunt.

Players at the turn of the century with a Glasgow and South Western train steaming towards Prestwick station *(courtesy of Prestwick Golf Club)*

The Golfers' Line and on to Turnberry!

If ever directors of a railway company were fully aware of the value of golf to their business, it will have been the Board of the Glasgow & South Western in the 1890s. They had the good fortune to operate the line between Glasgow and Ayr and their confidence knew no bounds.

In 1879 the previous generation of the Board had ensured the opening of Scotland's first railway hotel at Glasgow's St Enoch Station. Even the baronial touches could not hide the fact the design was based on London's St Pancras, with both abutting a train shed yet both undeniably lordly. Glasgow now had a handsome city terminal complete with luxurious accommodation for the traveller. In later years it was to win the affection of the Duke of Windsor and many popular singers of grand and light opera, including Caruso, Ivor Novello and the much loved Jack Buchanan. So that no one should doubt to whom they were indebted for such magnificence, the entrance hall of the hotel depicted the company's coat of arms in mosaic.

The Ayrshire coast can be damp and breezy but it is favoured with a fair weather belt in which many classic golf courses proliferate. In 1851 the trailblazer was Prestwick. It was succeeded in 1878 by Troon, by Barassie and Irvine in 1887, Glasgow Gailes in 1892 and then Western Gailes five years later. Many other less well-known links jostle the line, with the town of Troon accounting for another six, and Prestwick for two. Little wonder then that in 1910 the railway from Glasgow to Ayr was dubbed the 'The Golfers' Line' by *Rail and Travel Monthly* magazine.

Glasgow Gailes shared a private station with its neighbour Western Gailes. Both are country clubs for Glaswegians but the Glasgow club at Gailes is unique in having a sister course at Killermont. The Killermont members had the choice of site either to the east or west of the line. They opted for the east, possibly anticipating greater shelter but certainly conscious the level terrain would make for wonderful golfing country.

Within twenty years there was a wish to upgrade the Ayrshire course to be on a par with its rivals. Willie Park was at that time acquiring a reputation as a golf-course architect. Much of his work had been in his native Scotland although arguably the best examples of his skill are in England at Silloth, Sunningdale, and Huntercombe. Park remodelled Glasgow Gailes in 1911 from which he gained a lot of satisfaction, viewing it as one of his better efforts in his own country. His work here has stood the test of time. It offers natural golf devoid of artificiality or pretence. Winding among the ever-present gorse and heather is the traditional game such as Scotsmen have introduced the world over. Former Open Champion Sandy Lyle, a man of few words but great skill, has described it as one of the truly great tests and complementing it admirably is the Victorian clubhouse, recently renovated, and now a model of how to meld old and new.

West of the line lies Western Gailes. In open links land leased from the Duke of Portland and once used by the Irvine Volunteers as a shooting range, the course is sandwiched between the tracks and dunes that hide sands so massive they have long been popular for training race horses. The course overlooks the

Original watercolour by G. Drummond Fish of the first green at Western Gailes *c.*1937
(courtesy of Western Gailes Golf Club)

Isle of Arran whose mountains dominate the skyline forming a dramatic backcloth. To the south the lone crag of Ailsa Craig rises from the sea, and some 57 miles to the north the Paps of Jura can just be discerned.

The clubhouse stands on the site of an old horse-drawn tramway that ran from Irvine to Troon. Opened in 1812, three years before Wellington's victory over Napoleon at Waterloo, this was probably the first railway to carry coal.

From the outset Western Gailes was an immediate success despite being a temperance establishment. Within a couple of months 300 Glaswegians had signed up for the modest cost of half a guinea for the entrance fee, and the same again as an annual subscription. After only four years saturation point was reached with membership at 600, even though the entrance fee had escalated to seven guineas and the subscription had nearly tripled to a hefty £1 10s!

No club was ever as reliant on the railway. There is an implicit acknowledgement of this in the names of the first two holes – Station and Railway – for other than the station, sole and exclusive access to Western was via a level crossing. So when the motorcar came into vogue, the lucky man controlling the crossing from the nearby signal box held a coveted position: each driver tipped him in the hope of obtaining preferential treatment.

Since scarcely a member resided within 15 miles, the Glasgow & South Western Railway could well appreciate the club's dependence on them. Ready liaison with the clubmaster prompted him to ring a bell to warn of the approaching Glasgow train. Immediately drinks would be downed and conversation abandoned. Once aboard, early morning games of solo could be resumed with the intention of recuperating wagers lost on the links.

However sincere was their goodwill, it did not sully the railway's commercial instincts. When after ten years the club sought cheap return tickets, the stern reply from the St Enoch stationmaster was that no third-class return fares could be issued before noon. With first-class returns costing 3s 9d, a regular player could spend as much in six weeks' travel to play the game as he would on a year's subscription. This hard-nosed attitude towards golfers was at a time when railway companies were wooing all sorts of other organisations with concessionary fares. Typically, these included anglers, archers, the Band of Hope, billiard parties, the Boys Brigade, chess clubs, church choirs, and even handbell ringers!

Decades later British Rail went a stage further when they decided not to pay the level-crossing keeper on Sundays. As this would have deprived members of their only access, the club was literally forced to pick up the tab. In turn, to fund this players were invited to place half-a-crown in an honesty box, a practice which continued until the introduction of automatic signalling and control of the crossing. Of the station that was so vital to life at Gailes there is now no trace; services ceased in 1966 and few remember the role it once played.

Bookmarks produced by the GSWR for players of the game they knew so well
(courtesy of the National Railway Museum, York)

Strangely for an elitist establishment, yet one which has hosted the ladies' Curtis Cup between Britain and America, there is neither a professional nor a shop. There are no ladies' tees for there are no female members. Quietly but emphatically, this is a gentleman's club. Here one finds the steward wearing a morning suit. Little has changed over the years. Only the no alcohol rule has been revoked; and if you want to purchase golf balls, the man who served you a kümmel after lunch has them neatly stacked by the gin!

In 1925 *Golf at its Best on the LMS* captured the atmosphere of Western Gailes nicely. Many an English green was said to compare unfavourably to their tees. The course was the private cache of the Glasgow businessman and visitors without the necessary references were not encouraged. Delicately the author Del Leigh wrote how there was,

> none of the rush or scurry, or clamour of caddies, or sprinting to put a ball down. You are given the impression that the man who takes you there is taking you to his own golf course built especially for him in his own grounds.

With membership now little more than half what it was in 1901, the air of privilege is unmistakable as is the discreet *bonhomie*.

This atmosphere and the popularity of the game was well understood by the Glasgow & South Western Railway, especially as further down the line

Prestwick's prestige remained unchallenged in the west of Scotland. So it was in anticipation, and with confidence, that the directors applied to the Light Railway Commissioners in 1896 for permission to build a new line south of Ayr to Girvan under the romantic name of the Maidens & Dunure Light Railway.

Their dream was to establish at Turnberry the first ever golfers' hotel. Here the Marquess of Ailsa, a fellow director, had his own private thirteen-hole course which he was willing to sell. Together, the new hotel and upgraded course would offer justification for the new line. The Board also envisaged the railway would attract tourists in its own right as at speeds not exceeding 25mph passengers would enjoy the views at their leisure. After all, there was a stunning coastline, ancient castles and a countryside associated with Robbie Burns.

The commissioners were not people to be pressurised. They were painstaking and took three long years to agree. Two years later there was not one golf course but two, since the company had commissioned a full-length championship course for the men and a gentle nine holes for the ladies. The architect chosen to reconstruct the early layout was Willie Fernie, doyen of the famous Scottish golfing family, and former Open Champion.

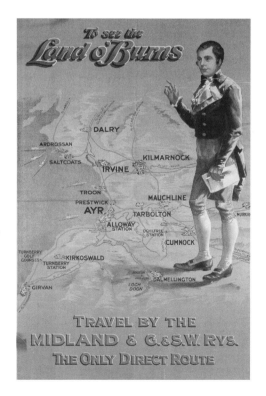

'Land o' Burns' poster *(courtesy of the National Railway Museum/Science & Society Picture Library)*

By now the Glasgow & South Western Railway's dream was five years old. As there was precious little to show for it, the company decided to act boldly and finalise their purchase in acquiring from the Marquess the land on which both courses stood. Unfettered they could now develop the country's first ever golfing holiday complex and steal a march on their competitors at Cruden Bay and Dornoch.

The eleventh hole on the Ailsa championship course at Turnberry
(courtesy of Turnberry Golf Club)

Suitably motivated, progress was to be orderly and on 17 May 1906 the ten-year-old plan came to fruition. Both the hotel and the new line opened together. With 131 bedrooms and twice the size of the Highland Railway's Station Hotel at Dornoch, the new hotel lived up to the company's claims. There were hot and sea water baths, billiards, bridge and the finest views anyone could wish for. On a good day, the sight of distant Arran embodied mystery and the quintessence of island romance while the nearer to hand, Ailsa Craig, home of gulls and guillemots, was a comforting landmark. Even in bad weather the scene was inspiring as Arran disappeared in the mist leaving Ailsa Craig like a remote primeval fortress, scarcely part of the real world at all. Each evening guests dressed for dinner and afterwards there was dancing. With facilities so comprehensive, aside from golf there was no need to leave the hotel grounds.

The company's foresight in planning and achieving a golf and leisure complex was commendable. However, their crystal ball was somewhat cloudy in forecasting the viability of the new line, named the Turnberry. Golfers alone could not support it and the volume of business generated by eleven country stations proved of little avail. After 25 years – the same lifespan of the line at Machrihanish – passengers lost their service.

By then the London Midland & Scottish Railway had long absorbed the Glasgow & South Western Railway. Appreciating that Turnberry's principal clientele were wealthy Londoners or Americans flying into the capital, at first they shrewdly retained the short stretch of line north of Girvan to Turnberry. This meant sleeper passengers could continue to enjoy a direct service before an undercover walk straight from the platform to the large conservatory at the rear of the hotel. But in February 1942 that line ceased operation too. The London market had dried up and the RAF took over a large part of the links. Rail services into Turnberry became a thing of the past.

After the war, the new generation in the LMS railway headquarters at Euston must have likened the Turnberry complex to an albatross. They laid on a bus from Kilmarnock station but it seemed scarcely the ideal way to treat first-class passengers. Yet a tiny cadre in British Transport Hotels was to think more positively. They recognised that unless the standards at Turnberry were superlative it would not survive. So they drew the finest chefs from London, Edinburgh and Glasgow, and soon the cuisine earned rosettes from Michelin and the accolades rivalled Gleneagles.

How long such extravagance could endure under a nationalised industry shackled with set accounting principles was doubtful. In 1969 Egon Ronay, that champion of excellence in the world of *haute cuisine*, had become scathing. He was critical of the waiters, calling them loud-mouthed and undisciplined; ignorant; devoid of skills. Somehow, however, the management's determination just won through; they succeeded in selling the hotel as a going concern and fortunately under successive new ownership it has thrived, regenerating the atmosphere of a grand Edwardian country house to count as one of the great hotels of the world.

As for the golf course, unlike a fine Rhone wine which may take a good 20 years to mature, Turnberry needed 70 years before it came of age. Twice in wartime it was requisitioned for conversion to an airport. Mercifully, each time restoration and improvement followed. In the 1950s, after all eight blind holes had been superseded and the expertise of architect Mackenzie Ross was beginning to show, it dawned on the authorities that here was a major links to rank alongside the very best in Britain with a setting that is incomparable. Today, defying its remote location, away from the main lines of communication, many commentators consider Turnberry to be the most glorious of Open venues.

This unlikely turn of events was partly due to fate. In 1977 the Royal & Ancient took a gamble in holding the Open there. Yet it paid off. In a heatwave, Turnberry set the scene of the epic shoot-out between Tom Watson and Jack Nicklaus. No one who saw this is likely to forget what has to be the most thrilling head-to-head encounter in the history of golf in Britain.

That first morning was breathless. As a speedboat with a water skier in tow skimmed across the bay, the effect was like a mirror cracking. Seasoned pundits were convinced the course would be torn apart. Rightly so, for from the start very low scores were posted, mainly by young Americans who were unknown in Britain. The passage of time has not improved their fame, since the pace they set was unsustainable under the pressure induced by Jack Nicklaus and Tom Watson.

Nicklaus was (and still is) widely regarded as the finest player the game of golf has seen. Tom Watson, already Open Champion once, looked like the one man who might conceivably dislodge him from his pedestal. With two neat halves of 34, Watson had a satisfying start, as did Nicklaus, who came storming home in 31 for a similar 68.

On the second day Watson had a short putt for a par at the first, but missed. His two 35s were steady but hardly inspiring. On the other hand, Nicklaus was intimidating, going out on 33. Then he fiddled on the greens and he, too, had a 70. It was the third round that separated the men from the boys. The young Americans began to falter while Nicklaus was ebullient, striking a miscellany of world-class strokes. Out in 31 he came home in 34. His 65 might have been a 63 or even 62. At the fourteenth, his ball shaved the cup and, temporarily unhinged, he failed with the easy one back to record his only 5 of the day. Then at the seventeenth after a quite masterly number two iron he was unable to pop the ball in from four feet.

Meanwhile Watson, who was partnering him for the first time, took nothing more than a 4. His 33 out and 32 back, with a couple of twos at the fourth and fifteenth, was near perfection. The two of them were still tied, now three shots ahead of Ben Crenshaw, and with Watson appearing to be the more complete golfer, the smarter sages looked to him for the winner.

Nicklaus was never more determined. He started his last round 4 3 4 2, and after forty minutes was now three ahead. The riposte was not long coming. In the next four holes Watson scored three birdies to draw level. Nicklaus clawed one back at the lighthouse hole, and with a killer birdie at the twelfth was once more two ahead.

Again the pendulum swung. Watson counter-attacked with a birdie at the 411-yard thirteenth. It galvanised him. Lithe and radiant, he now strode to the fifteenth where his confidence was rewarded. A monster putt from the edge of the green rattled into the hole. Back to level once again. Then they halved the sixteenth. The seventeenth is 500 yards long. Here Nicklaus was jolted for Watson's iron was a pearl, coming to rest in the heart of the green. Nicklaus collected himself to play a deft pitch then his composure wavered and he missed an easy four-footer.

Watson now had the lead for the first time. Choosing an iron from the eighteenth tee, his ball hugged the corner of the dog-leg before rolling into prime position on the fairway. He stood back and waited. The pressure was on Nicklaus and it showed. Peter Thomson was in the commentator's box. A five-time winner of the Open, he was the ideal person to convey the excitement to those watching the drama unfold on television. For the only time on this tee all week, Nicklaus reached for his driver. Prophetically Thomson prefaced the blow in his Australian twang that it was 'Sydney or the Bush'. Giving an almighty clout, Nicklaus succumbed to that occasional weakness of his and came off the shot. The ball drifted to the right. Fulfilling Thomson's prophecy it came to rest under the edge of a gorse bush. Another turn or so and he would have had no option but to hack out sideways. Putting on his bravest face, Nicklaus stooped to examine the lie then, standing tall to select a line, he breathed deep and played a recovery beyond the aspirations of his most ardent fans. Gasps of amazement were drowned by applause as the ball landed on a corner of the green.

Now the spotlight was on Watson; he selected a 7 iron and without ceremony drilled it on line to within a yard of the hole. This was the ultimate *coup de grâce* of any Open. Though Watson smiled he did not permit himself a quiet pat on the back. He prepared himself for the unexpected, knowing his work was not yet done.

Nicklaus had one more card to play. From almost out of sight of the hole, the man recognised the world over as the Golden Bear had the gall to hole the putt. One minute the ball had looked inextricable, the next his birdie appeared inexplicable. The crowd went wild before order was restored; silence followed as each held his breath.

Watson blinked, steeled himself, and holed out straight as a die for the half in 3 and, with it, a 65 against 66. There were cheers. In 117 years there had never been anything quite like it. Those privileged to be present knew they had witnessed history.

It is indelicate to recall it but at one time Watson had been considered a quitter. No longer. From this day on he never looked back. The metamorphosis of Turnberry and Tom Watson was now complete. In the next six years he won the Open three more times – at Muirfield, Troon and Royal Birkdale. Nicklaus, too, continued to grow in stature. The following year at St Andrews it was his turn again to receive the old claret jug.

Further Opens at Turnberry have produced champions of similar ilk. On each occasion the drama has been intense and, more than that, it would be a fair claim to say that each winner at that moment in time was the best player in the world.

Were there ever to be a call to hold the Open at only one course, in just the same way the U.S. Masters is confined to Augusta, any claims put forward for Turnberry would be hard to resist. Turnberry invites theatre. This is big country where the leading players act out their role like the stars they are.

Formerly the fanciful creation of a Marquess that was then nurtured by Glasgow railwaymen, it is fascinating to see how their judgement was as clear as a bell when it came to golf. More so, alas, than when they chose to extend the still very successful Golfers' Line between Glasgow and Ayr to Turnberry.

Machrihanish – the Playground

Machrihanish is both one of the most remarkable golf courses that Scotland has to offer, and one of its best-preserved secrets. Situated on the rugged west coast of the Kintyre peninsula, inaccessibility is part of the attraction. The casual visitor does not feature: those who take the trouble to visit mostly know what they are about but are not necessarily aware that, at the turn of the century, for Glasgow's well-to-do it was known as 'The Playground'.

Evidence of old moneyed interests can still be seen in the handsome villas gazing seaward over the eighteenth hole. Prosperous Victorians had built them as holiday homes. Life had been good here and black-tie dinners were regular events. Among the club captains before the Great War were members of the Coats dynasty, founders of the worldwide thread business.

As for the golf course it is the most natural place to play one could possibly imagine. It was primarily the creation of Old Tom Morris of St Andrews and Prestwick fame, although in all modesty he preferred to say that 'Machrihanish was designed by the Almighty'.

Opposite the entrance to the clubhouse the first tee stands proud by the ocean. Over one's shoulder are rocks caressed by the swell where seals bask limply. Ahead the drive has to carry the corner of a crescent of silver sand; seemingly endless and pristine, either it is lapped by spume or assaulted by rollers. Many writers and, indeed, course designers rate this as the finest opening hole in the game. Yet that would be a euphemism, for the first three make the most enchanting start one could conceive.

By now one is among sand dunes, aiming to fire the tee shot with the accuracy of a rifle: otherwise twin alternatives are equally unpalatable – either massive grassy hummocks or vast sandy bunkers. Only then will there be a realistic opportunity to flight the second shot so that the ball will stop on greens which present either an undulating bowl or a slippery parapet.

At the tenth one turns to face the prevailing wind. No matter what the outward score is, the real business of coping with the grandeur and the elements commences in earnest. The test is unrelenting, as holes dodge between dunes at varying angles and dog-legs confuse. Only at the last is there any let up since a well-judged pitch offers a birdie chance. A quick glance at the card may have indicated the course is not long by modern standards, but that is to mislead, for both finesse and strength are required in abundance.

Machrihanish is the most westerly course on the Scottish mainland; and it used to be the terminus for a singular little railway which ran from Campbeltown harbour to the Ugadale Arms. Converted into holiday flats, the building is now shorn of pride, but in the 1950s and 60s its ambience was gracious in the style of a rather grand, though not particularly large, railway hotel. There was an imposing staircase, potted palms, and a pleasing decor of cream and white, green and gold. Sunday lunch included the option of a colonial-style curry, or a gargantuan cold buffet, with no limit to the number of times one could help oneself. A well-stocked bar contained specialist malts from Islay, visible a few miles to the north west. Scots and English voices spoke in cultured tones and serenity reigned. Here was a hotel that advertised discreetly in the personal column of *The Times* to which guests were to return time and again.

It was in 1876 that the building of the line commenced and the first few holes of the golf course were laid out. A Campbeltown minister cut the first sod. Ten holes were built and the rules of golf in force at Prestwick were adopted. Making no charge for his land, the farmer could play for free. Charlie Hunter, professional at Prestwick, soon recommended the course be changed to 12 holes and three years later Old Tom Morris extended this to eighteen.

In 1877 the founding minister became ill and it was feared he would die. However, he recovered, played in the autumn meeting and was elected captain the following year. He lived on until 1921, eloquent testimony to golf's therapeutic value.

The original purpose of the railway was to convey coal from a colliery on the Duke of Argyll's land at Kilkivan to a railhead in Campbeltown. Spasmodic mining had taken place for some years, but cartage into town at 2s 6d per ton was a high proportion of the coal's local selling price of 6s 8d. In contrast, rail transit would reduce the cartage element for the final leg of the journey to just 6d per ton. Furthermore, it was foreseen that with a new shaft being sunk other markets might be tackled, since production could be stepped up beyond what the local market of 8,000 people and 20 distilleries (in due course to reach 35) was able to absorb. Indeed coal exports to Scandinavia and Prussia were to commence via schooners from Campbeltown quay.

By the turn of the century, a whole new business had sprung up. Thousands of day-trippers and holidaymakers arrived in Kintyre from Clydeside on the railway company-owned paddle-steamers. Between 1901 and 1903, 136,000 passengers came to Campbeltown, of which some 22,000 were conveyed to Machrihanish on horse-drawn charabancs. The challenge to the little railway company was clear and it responded.

In the spring of 1905 it secured a Light Railway order. A few weeks later a prospectus intimated that the new Association of Argyll Railway Company would take over from both the Campbeltown Coal Company and the light railway. The line was to be extended to the harbour quay in Campbeltown, so putting paid to the carters running to the water's edge from the town depot, while simultaneously enabling the volume of coal exports to be increased dramatically. The line was then to be extended in the west to Machrihanish golf club and the Ugadale Arms. The Campbeltown Coal Company subscribed for shares in the new company, which was to be called the Campbeltown and Machrihanish Light Railway Company. Other shareholders included the builders of the turbine paddle-steamers and local distillers. The concept seemed a sure-fire winner and a profit of 5.7 per cent return on capital of £26,000 was forecast.

Passenger services began the following year. The venture looked gilt-edged since in the first three weeks 10,000 people took advantage of the service. 'The Playground' was now rail connected and the little train of green and white

Campbeltown Quay and terminus *(courtesy of David Thomas)*

The Golfers' Express *(courtesy of Dalkeith Picture Postcards)*

coaches, averaging 12.5mph and hauled by the locomotive Argyll, acquired the tag of 'the Golfer's Express'. The golf club was so delighted that the Scottish Ladies were invited to hold their championship in 1909. It was voted such a success they returned in 1913, and twice more in the twenties.

The railway went from strength to strength. To appease golfers, the last train off Machrihanish at 17.10 was put back to 18.30. A one-coach train ran to suit the colliery shifts, another met the needs of schoolchildren and, briefly, there was a milk train. There were football specials, troop trains for Territorial Army summer camps in the dunes backing on to the links, and steamer expresses. The railway had ousted the horse-drawn charabanc business.

Though isolated, the little railway prospered and its success was noted. One company alive to the prospect of integrating it into the main network was the Glasgow & South Western Railway. By 1910, like both the Caledonian Railway and the North British Railway, it too had diversified and now owned a number of paddle-steamers. It wanted to be allowed in at Campbeltown for regular sailings rather than just for excursions.

Their vision was to construct a railway going right down to the south of the peninsula linking into the light railway from Machrihanish to Campbeltown. The plan included ownership of a new hotel at Bellochantuy and another golf course facing on to Gigha that would rival Machrihanish and the more southerly Dunaverty. The intention was to take over the C&MLR, so securing access to Campbeltown and acquiring a stranglehold on exports through it and the other lesser ports. Except for whisky, the railway company aimed to dominate the Kintyre economy.

Progress was halted by the Great War and in 1919 the matter was considered again. One ambitious plan was to take the railway north, from just south of Machrihanish, to Lochgilphead and Inveraray, joining the Highland Railway at Crianlarich. But the local Rural Transport District Committee was biased towards road and so bus companies were formed. Immediately, they were favoured by the Royal Mail who chose that moment to disband their vehicle fleet and put their business out to contract.

The following year the Campbeltown colliery went on strike. Nine years later it ceased production altogether. That left the railway to survive on passenger traffic alone. To augment the frequency of services, the C&MLR bought a couple of buses but these regularly broke down. Bus competition from local operators became more intense and, although the trains retained their popularity for summer excursions, once the season ended passenger demand dwindled.

During the winter of 1931/32 the rolling stock was laid up for two months. When schedules were due to resume it was found that expensive repairs had become necessary. Sadly, if inevitably, the funds available were insufficient for the purpose and, with steamers arriving, holidaymakers had no option but to resort to bus. The last whistle had blown on the railway. After just 25 years the service had quietly petered out. The sure-fire gilt-edged venture had collapsed just like countless other well-intentioned private railway undertakings.

On the other hand, golf at Machrihanish has survived with a certain buoyancy which is contagious. Happily the course remains a marvel. Visiting parties fly in for the day from Glasgow. Their high expectations are exceeded. Meantime the morning bus from Campbeltown acts as reminder of the little railway since in school holidays small boys dismount armed with golf bags, all chattering away like monkeys as they make a beeline for the first tee of the short nine-hole course. Holes still have names. The fourteenth – Castlehill – commemorates that Campbeltown minister of the Castlehill Church of Scotland, who had such an impact on the first 45 years of the club. There is an air that nothing has changed or is likely to. Oystercatchers continue to patrol the links in confidence and at ease, sharing their playground with members of a club who honour their species in having it as their much-loved symbol.

Should there be a golf course in heaven, may it be like Machrihanish. After all, as Old Tom Morris declared, it was designed by the Almighty!

Machrihanish

Edwardian summer days would see,
But barely seven miles away,
Packed steamers call at Campbeltown
With Glasgow folk on holiday.

There used to be a railway
To Machrihanish via the plain,
Its cargo principally coal
Or tourists on the golfers' train.

Neat villas gazing seawards bear
Reminder of those well-heeled Scots
Who owned a summer sanctuary
Far off from moneyed honeypots.

Their view, so valued by these men,
Remains the same as yesteryear—
Beyond untrammelled silver sands
The Paps of Jura, Islay, Gigha.

But much has changed: no coal is mined,
No longer do the Boys Brigade
Parade the dunes at summer camp
To hunt for golf balls as they strayed.

Still, oystercatchers strut and delve
Where Canterbury bells grow free
Delighting players young and old,
At peace as in eternity.

Royal Dornoch – an Inspiration

Ask any enthusiast to name a Scottish links that has been the adulation of the very finest players in Britain and America, and the odds are the answer will be Royal Dornoch.

Dornoch's success became a byword early on. In the 1890s it encouraged the Glasgow & South Western Railway to develop a golf complex at Turnberry and construct a lengthy line to it. By that time, solely on account of the draw of its golf, Dornoch had its own branch line. For Donald Matheson of the Caledonian Railway, creator of Gleneagles, it was his inspiration as well as the competitor he attempted to humble.

The club was formed in 1877, although for some 300 years the game had been played there informally. In the seventeenth century it was described as 'the fairest of any pairt of Scotland' and earlier still, in 1570, it was where the Bishop of Caithness and Sutherland would regularly spend 'the Kirk's rents at the golf and guid chier'. While clergy and golf have long enjoyed a connection, especially in Ireland, this must be the first record of a prelate under rebuke because of the game and the conviviality that followed!

Dornoch enjoys an enviable setting above the firth. The cathedral and town, with its ordered sandstone castle and broad streets, bespeak a rich thoughtfulness. A short walk from the centre brings one to the links. They nestle between a mile-long escarpment of brilliant yellow gorse, and secretive dunes which cosset the finest possible sinuous sands for miles around. The scene from the third tee is awe-inspiring and it continues to be so until the end of the course.

Golf at Dornoch was to precede the dramatic growth in the game of the late 1880s. In 1879 there were only 98 courses in Britain. By 1890 the tally was 375; and in the decade that followed the pace accelerated further. Prior to this the railway network had also been expanding fast. The 1,500 route miles of 1837 had grown ten-fold by 1870, then reached 20,000 by 1890 – double the size of today. Where the tracks had led, golf was following. Conversely,

Dornoch having been bypassed, was suffering hard times. The nearest station was ten miles away at Tain across the firth, and to get there was quite a feat for it required a coach and horses on both sides of the Meikle Ferry. Nowadays, a curious signpost points to 'Meikle Ferry North (no ferry)'!

The man who turned the situation around was the club's young secretary, John Sutherland. Due to his efforts Dornoch was elevated from beyond the fringe to a golfing centre in its own right. He foresaw that prosperity ought to follow in the wake of the railways, so in preparation he invited Old Tom Morris of St Andrews to design 'nine proper holes'. Later he was to add nine more himself and promote the whole in *Golf Illustrated* and various London newspapers.

Meanwhile, the Highland Railway Board was alive to what was going on and could appreciate Dornoch's potential as a holiday resort. The catalyst for change was the 1896 Railways Act which permitted local lines to be constructed to less exacting standards than main routes. In being cheaper, an economic case was easier to justify. The following year the Dornoch Light Railway Company was formed under the chairmanship of the Duke of Sutherland. Very sensibly the Duke then persuaded the Highland Railway that both would benefit if they were to build the branch on his company's behalf. It duly opened, in June 1902, on a miserable wet day before a crowd of 1,000, and ran from the Mound south of Golspie, past the fishing village of Embo and skirting the seventh and eighth holes into the little town.

Bunkers in front of the eighteenth green with Royal Dornoch clubhouse in the distance
(courtesy of Royal Dornoch Golf Club)

As part of the overall plan the Highland Railway commissioned the luxury Station Hotel 300 yards from the terminus. This opened two years later and, at £30,000, cost the same as the seven-mile branch line. Targeted on golfers and their families, the 65-bedroomed hotel included a billiard room, hairdressing salon in polished oak and black-and-white tiles, a golfers' corner with bar, and several private sitting rooms. A special feature was the 16 HP generator which provided the hotel's own electricity.

Holidays in the Scottish Highlands had now become the height of fashion as Queen Victoria's love of the area was emulated by the wealthy. So once a Pullman car from Euston had been introduced to the service, Dornoch presented a more attractive destination, despite the 636-mile journey from London. One could now dine off crested china bearing the railway company's insignia, and be fortified by serious clarets or good hock. Slumbering between clean linen sheets, one might awaken to the sight of sun-splashed mountain streams before succumbing to a mammoth breakfast in the Cairngorms at Kingussie. Later there would be glimpses of the sea lapping on dimpled sands, and the majesty of the Atlantic fleet calmly at anchor within the Cromarty Firth. The train lent enchantment – a happy prelude to the holiday itself.

As a young man Bernard Darwin was greatly given to rail travel and he summed the sensation up:

> Is it altogether too shameful an admission that one of the pleasantest things about the night journey to Scotland is to lie in your bunk and hear the clanking of milk cans and the scurrying feet along the platform and hug to yourself the knowledge that you are safe in your own little kingdom?

The wealthier visitors to Dornoch were now following Lord Rothermere's example and building themselves a villa. American millionaire and philanthropist, steel magnate Andrew Carnegie went one better. He created his dream castle and private nine-hole golf course in a magical setting on the firth, not five miles away at Skibo. Here he entertained famous lawyers, bankers and artists and talented friends.

One of these was J. H. Taylor, three times Open Champion, then at the height of his powers and inspiration. Twice more he was to win the Open. In the mornings Taylor gave lessons to the rich and their wives. None was keener than Carnegie. After lunch he made sure his time was spent even more satisfactorily in playing all-comers for hefty wagers. No matter how generous the stroke allocation he agreed to concede, he knew well enough how such monetary pressure would encourage his opponents into error. Large sums found their way into his back pocket as a matter of routine, with all concerned delighted at his golfing genius and the losers feeling strangely honoured.

This was the dawn of a golden era for in 1906 King Edward VII, a close friend of the third Duke of Sutherland, granted the club a royal charter. By now the country's best golfers were making tracks for Dornoch. Among them were Taylor's fellow members of the Great Golfing Triumvirate, Harry Vardon and James Braid.

All relished the atmosphere and the challenge of Dornoch's forbidding short holes. The first three, namely the second, sixth and tenth, are each more difficult than the world-renowned Postage Stamp at Royal Troon. Each man recognised, too, the necessity for accurate shots into the greens, since to miss either to the left or right calls for a degree of artistry which is granted to few. It is a course where talent alone is insufficient. Patience and wiliness are essential if a respectable score is to be pieced together.

Royal Dornoch's growing fame was not confined to this side of the Atlantic. Two of the town's young men were making a name for themselves in the USA. Alec Ross won the U.S. Open in 1907, while his brother Donald was establishing a career of longer lasting fame. He became the outstanding golf-course architect of his age. Designing more than 500, he is best remembered for Pinehurst Number Two. One of his tricks was to create an elevated green, then to surround it with bunkers as though it were a crown adorned with jewels. It was a direct crib from the Dornoch of Old Tom Morris and John Sutherland, the feature that so beguiles and infuriates, and renders a medal round tough beyond belief.

After the Great War the golden era of those Edwardian days resumed as if there had been no interruption. For some time the banker H. N. Wethered had owned a holiday house. Golf was in his blood. His daughter Joyce, less than robust, was taught at home by a governess. Adept at golf, she was encouraged to practise. Her elder brother Roger, a devotee destined to become one of the great amateur players between the wars, goaded her in exasperation, 'Oh, Joyce, you will never play golf. You won't study the game'. He had a point for apparently she only ever had two lessons!

Joyce spent her childhood holidays in this charged environment, and in the boisterous school of brother Roger and his pals she acquired her proficiency and poise. The Wethered house backed on to the links, and Joyce commented, 'We had merely to cross the road and drop over a low wall to find ourselves in front of the big bunker which for so many years had defeated our best drives on the second tee'. How modest of her – for the second is that first short hole!

The custom at the time was for all golfers to have caddies. Men, boys and girls were happy to hump others' bags and get fun from the experience. The caddies had a field day in adopting nicknames for the diverse and talented English visitors: a slow old gent was called 'the Curse of Scotland'; an aquiline Oxonian was 'the Vulture' (pronounced 'Vultuah'); an irascible codger was 'Old

Damn and Blast', and a Scottish international who took every ill rub of the green as a gross personal misfortune, exclaiming violently 'crushing luck' quite regardless of the evidence, was of course 'Crushing Luck'. But Joyce was simply Joyce and was looked on in awe by the girl caddies from the fishing town of Embo, a few miles to the north.

Joyce played not only at Dornoch. She and Roger visited all the top courses within an hour or two in distance away. She broke the course record on her first visit to Brora, and was well known at Golspie, Nairn, and the Moray Club at Lossiemouth where the sandy trap by the elevated third green is still known as Joyce Wethered's bunker. The tee then was way behind the road and the hole considerably longer than the present 400 yards. No matter that she played with hickory shafts, such was Joyce's timing that she put her second into the greenside bunker. Even now it seems hardly credible. Little wonder she was welcomed wherever she went in Ross-shire and along the Moray Firth Riviera. The prowess of this teenage girl, loyal to her cloche hat with its off-the-face brim, was such that caddies would bet their boots on her winning, taking all kinds of money off unsuspecting visitors.

When only 18 years old, she entered for the English Ladies championship in 1920 at middle-class Sheringham to keep her friend Molly Griffiths company. Molly led the qualifiers but in a cold Norfolk breeze Joyce struggled and just scraped into the knockout format with an unhappy 94. Not an auspicious beginning to the world of ladies tournament golf! In the first round proper Molly was plagued with three-putting and lost, whereas Joyce was getting the hang of things and sailed through by 7/6. In the second round, with her confidence soaring, she slaughtered her poor opponent by 8/6 to reach the final.

This match was far more formidable, her opposition being Cecil Leitch, the most talented of five golfing sisters from Silloth in Cumbria. Cecil was 'the big noise' in ladies golf; the following year she was to win the Canadian ladies title by annihilating her opponent 17/15, a record to this day for a formal 36-hole match.

Cecil thwacked the ball, swinging fast, and in throwing her all into it from a wide stance achieved a sudden motion like a whirling dervish dancer. Appearing purposeful and sporting a characteristic bandanna, she looked like, and was, a warm and popular favourite. Four up at lunch, by the twenty-first Cecil had advanced to a lead of 6 up and seemed unassailable when still 4 to the good with nine holes remaining. Then came a string of sensational figures from Joyce, which turned Cecil's world upside down.

The ground was baked hard as a board, and with the wind behind and a downhill gradient both girls were capable of quite astonishing length. Joyce's drive found the middle of the twelfth green 296 yards away, to secure the

Joyce Wethered at Sheringham, 1920, watched by an apprehensive Cecil Leitch on her
way to victory and the start of her extraordinary career
(*courtesy of Mr and Mrs L. D. Blunden*)

second of her three consecutive 3s. Resolutely refusing even to glance at Cecil
in fear of being affected by the other's ungainly rhythm, Joyce clawed her way
back into the match immersed in a cocoon of concentration. She was swinging
divinely, beautifully balanced, her weight on her heels, clearing her left hip out
of the way after impact, then following through high and wide with her right
arm pointing over her shoulder skywards. Yet it was not until the sixteenth hole
in the afternoon, thanks to a thrilling third shot, that she took the lead for the
first time. History was in the making.

The seventeenth green then was situated right by the railway line. Cecil
bunkered her second, extricated it, though not so well that Joyce didn't have two
shots for victory. Far from dead after 3, in the next moment a train went puffing

by. Unperturbed, Joyce did the business for victory by 2/1. Afterwards she claimed she never heard it. 'What train?' she enquired, a phrase the golfing world has never forgotten.

'What concentration', wrote Bernard Darwin sometime later. He understood the incident had occurred at Troon, while others thought St Andrews. Much later Joyce herself could shed little light on the matter though confessed that the 'What train?' episode must have been at Sheringham, since she connected it to an unfortunate whooping cough virus contracted there. That miserable spell had kept her on the sidelines for three months afterwards.

Joyce won the English Ladies Championship for the next four successive years. She mowed down her opposition, winning at Royal Lytham by 12/11, at Hunstanton by 7/6, and at Ganton and Cooden Beach both by 8/7. At Lytham she is remembered as being shy and reserved. She never practised, never sought to be 'one of the girls' and, after play, left as she came, in a Rolls Royce. Quite simply she was in a different league.

In 1922 and 1924 she captured the Ladies Amateur title, open to all. Again the margin of her victories was overwhelming – 9/7 at Princes against the unfortunate Cecil Leitch, then 7/6 at Royal Portrush in Northern Ireland. In 1925 at Troon, on her way to the Ladies Final with Cecil for the second time in four years, she was involved in yet another train incident. Joyce was up against America's top player, Glenna Collett. The match was proving extremely tight and after nine holes she was just one to the good. However, she won the tenth, and at the next, with an engine snorting right behind her, Joyce faced a long curly putt for a birdie which would then most likely put her 3 up. Since smoke was wafting over the green, she could not help but be aware of it; however her experience of Scottish golf held her in good stead. She sensed the driver would probably wait to see the hole completed before continuing on to Ayr with his goods. Hence, she got on with it and to gasps from the gallery saw the ball drop into the hole for the birdie. Both the driver and Joyce proceeded merrily on their ways. After winning by 4/3 she explained rationally that there would have been little to gain by waiting, for the driver's patience would have outlasted hers.

In 1929 she was to win the Ladies Amateur once more, at the home of golf, St Andrews. In all she played in eleven national championships. Once she was a finalist and once a semi-finalist, the other nine she was the winner. Her record is unique and bolstered by the fact that in the English Ladies, and British and French Ladies Opens, she played 82 rounds, winning 78. Of these 55 ended on or before the fourteenth green.

Having early cut her teeth on playing with and against men at Dornoch, Joyce took particular pleasure in the prestige event of autumn, the Worplesdon Foursomes. This was a mixed tournament that attracted the top names of the day. Joyce dominated it, winning eight times between 1922 and 1936, firstly with her brother and thereafter, except for scoring twice with Cyril Tolley, always with a different partner. In 1932 the lucky man was Raymond Oppenheimer, and in 1933, a grateful and elated Bernard Darwin (once chastened 6/5 by Joyce when the Ladies took on the Men at West Hill in 1924). It was Joyce's presence which always added lustre to the occasion, and many were the golfing couples for miles around who made this a firm date in their diaries as early as January.

What emerged from these tales of Joyce is how she won the esteem of the very best male players of her generation. Henry Cotton, three times Open Champion, and never one to lavish compliments where they were not deserved, questioned whether she was not the best player ever – male or female. After the war when she had long retired, it was said of her swing how much there was in common with Ben Hogan at his best, 'beautifully wide both on the back swing and also on the forward swing. She made no early hit, she had no wrist flick, and she kept a perfect centre.'

She even won the adulation of Bobby Jones in 1930, the year of his Grand Slam. After playing in a friendly fourball with her at St Andrews, he was dazzled and later wrote:

> she did not miss one shot; she did not even half miss one shot; and when we finished I could not help saying I had never played golf with anyone, man or woman, amateur or professional, who had made me feel so utterly outclassed . . . It was not so much the score she made (75) as the way she made it . . . It was impossible to expect that Miss Wethered would ever miss a shot – and she never did.

He never faltered in his admiration for her, saying 'I have found many people agree with me that Miss Wethered's swing was the most perfect in the world'. 'Rhythmic in the last degree', is how he described it.

For all this it was Royal Dornoch, where she was originally inspired, which was Joyce's favourite course.

Roger, too, five times winner of the President's Putter at Rye, struck the pinnacle. He remained one of the foremost British amateurs for more than 15 years. In 1921 he would have won the Open at St Andrews and been the first non-professional to do so since Harold Hilton in 1897, had he not trodden on his ball in third round and called a penalty on himself of a stroke. He was playing marvellously well and making up ground. After his initial 78 he had steadily improved scoring 75, 72 and 71. This tied him with American Professional Champion Jock Hutchison, on whom fate had smiled for he had holed in one at the eighth. In the pressure of the play-off Hutchison's professional experience saw him through. Over 36 holes Roger faltered to a nine shot deficit. However, compensation came two years later when he won the Amateur Championship.

If Royal Dornoch was fortunate in claiming the admiration of the Wethereds, none would gainsay it was other than deserving. From its earliest days onwards it attracted the discerning. The Station Hotel duly played its part in setting the tone by welcoming the well-to-do and socially acceptable, and having for hire a Rolls Royce.

Year after year quiet families of means and repute chose to return, with the ladies fondly remembering the final touch that on departure the manager would personally select for each a bud rose as a buttonhole. Sadly such gracious days ran out of time. In the mid 1960s, Beeching axed the branch and the hotel was sold. The murals in the dining room, redolent of the decor in ocean liners, seem out of place. Coach passengers on a one-night stopover have little time to reflect on the artistic inspiration behind Beatrice McDermott's painting of 'The Story of the Seasons', recounting the Greek myth of Persephone and Demeter.

In contrast, the American connection lives on. As with five-times Open Champion Tom Watson, Dornoch is for many the first call when starting on a golfing holiday in Britain and every August the American entry for the Carnegie Shield, that most treasured of the club's silver trophies, is extremely healthy.

Perhaps the greatest compliment to be paid Dornoch was by Ben Crenshaw. Gentle Ben, as he is known, is twice the winner of the U.S. Masters and an avid golfing historian. Preferring to play there than to practise for the Open he was asked how he got on. 'Let me put it this way', he replied, 'I nearly did not come back.'

Dornoch has this effect on people. It acts like a magnet. You may not now hear cries of, 'What train?' for rail is now an irrelevancy, but when that was the accepted mode of travel, like its most famous protégé, Joyce Wethered, it afforded a perfect centre. If Dornoch has been blessed in the choice of admirers, it is because of the inspiration it provides to the masterly and, in the case of the Bishop of Caithness and Sutherland, to the masterful too. For many it remains 'the fairest of any pairt of Scotland'.

The Glory of the Far North

Royal Dornoch may be the most celebrated links in the north of Scotland but it is no oasis. Three other courses worth a trek from the other side of the world are Golspie, Brora and Tain. Golspie, with its austere main street, seems an unlikely home town for the Duke of Sutherland. But appearances deceive and it is protected by pleasant woodland behind which lie purple hills. Dominating these is a monument to the controversial duke who authorised the Highland Clearances and, like it or not, it does serve as a timeless reminder of a very fraught period in our history.

From this vantage point the view is breathtaking. The railway resembles a model train set and the golf course appears petite, at the mercy of the sea. To the east, nestling on the far shores of the Dornoch Firth is the village of Portmahomack while, deep in the distance beyond the Moray Firth, the outline of Ben Rinnes can be discerned fully fifty miles away.

Rather like Golspie itself the character of the golf course is not immediately obvious. Yet although not unique, it is most unusual in that, like Grantown, it contains three very different elements – seaside links merge with holes on the heath (evocative of Berkshire at its most select) and meadowland; and throughout there is hardly a hole from which the sea is not readily visible.

At first glance Golspie offers a treeless expanse of greenery where the boisterous can open their shoulders. Yet as with the very best of golf courses there is a premium on accuracy and every incentive to place the ball with care. Otherwise the strokes simply melt away.

The challenge to the golfer begins immediately: a demanding shot to the first green is followed by a challenging tee shot to the second where the line is the chapel finial since the wide and undulating green is well hidden. Never other than a torment on which to two-putt, to land on the surface is better by far than a descent into one of several bunkers overhung with bents.

It is on leaving the insidious seventh green, when in all probability a birdie chance has gone begging, that one searches for superlatives. The dog-leg eighth

The fairytale Dunrobin Castle *(author's photograph)*

ushers in a new world reminiscent of Gleneagles or Sunningdale and, rightly, the ninth is called 'Paradise'. Severely exacting, it curves right to left with a switchback for a fairway amenable only to a shot like an arrow, or a gentle draw of the type at which Bobby Locke excelled. On either side lie heathery wastes. Those on the left are impenetrable. Towards the green, two bunkers are staggered and both beckon open-mouthed like a pair of hippopotami. With further terror behind the pin, correct club selection requires inspiration. All in all, this is arguably the best ninth hole in Britain.

Later, interspersed with parkland, come two short holes back-to-back in the dunes. The sixteenth is equally as awesome as the seventh at Rye though without the hell-hole of a bunker to carry. Instead, one is confronted with Braid's design of three tiers: an elevated double plateau green perched on a bank. The thrill of a good shot here exceeds every expectation, mirroring the infinite variety of the course itself.

A mile to Golspie's north the fairytale castle of Dunrobin can be found in a peerless setting. High on the headland above sunken parterre gardens and a three wood shot away from the sea, the Sutherlands would entertain royalty together with titled and distinguished friends.

One duke had his own train which he and his party would use when vacating London to take up summer residence. Opposite the castle gates and discreet as a forest lodge, is the little black-and-white station, formerly used by the gentry but now a simple request halt. Queen Victoria also enjoyed Dunrobin though naturally she travelled in her own train to be met by the duke with coach and horses.

A few miles further along the coast is the archetypal small Scottish resort of Brora. For generations it was known for the salmon from the river of the same name. This ran from Loch Brora into the charming little harbour that was commissioned by the first Duke of Sutherland as early as 1820. Nineteen years later it was the scene of sadness and trauma when crofters and their families, whom the duke had cleared, were to bid farewell to the north as they sailed to London on their way to a new life in New Zealand. Big ships could not be entertained as the scouring action of the currents causes the river mouth to silt up. The harbour was, however, haven to fishing smacks at the height of the herring boom some fifty years on.

The herring business required the support of a number of trades, each one dependent upon the other, and this explains the close-knit nature of Brora and other fishing communities. The skills involved included salters who cured the fish, coopers who made barrels in which the herring were conveyed to market, blacksmiths who fashioned iron bands to bind the barrels, and caulkers who maintained the hulls of the smacks in good repair.

Salt was captured in salt pans just south of the town but obtaining the ice posed a greater problem. This had to be cut by hand from frozen lochs high on the hills, then brought by horse and cart down potholed tracks to the Ice House at the harbour.

For well over a century there has been more to Brora than fishing. The riverbanks between the harbour and the sea are sandy and sheltered. Where the river reaches the sea, acres of rock pools offer fascination. In turn these are succeeded by untrammelled sands that flank dunes which run the entire length of the golf course. The beach shelves gently, so when warmed by the summer sun the sea, too, is hospitable.

Brora's links run for some two miles between the shore and the railway. The clubhouse is at the southern end and central to the town. The course was opened in 1892 by the Duchess of Sutherland, who, with her inaugural drive, missed the ball altogether! Her hickory-shafted club had a thick grip and its engraved silver blade certainly seems too precious for serious action. It is now on display at Dunrobin's garden museum, although tact has inhibited any reference to the air shot!

The success of golf at Brora is due in part to its pedigree and in part to its setting. Initially the course consisted of nine holes carved out by Dornoch's John Sutherland. Five years after the merriment surrounding that inauspicious opening ceremony, another nine were added. Then in 1905 came complete redesign.

J. H. Taylor was on holiday at Dornoch with his influential friends and came across for a game. On his advice 13 new greens were built and the orthodox layout of a loop was substituted for the original figure of eight. This survived for 18 years. Then with Brora fighting to hold its own against Dornoch, the top architect of the day, James Braid, was consulted. He arrived in the morning, walked the course, and took the next train back. Within the month his plans were approved, but he did not leave it there. He paid a second visit when he suggested further refinements and this is the design which gives such pleasure today.

From the course's early days the Highland Railway had promoted Brora willingly enough. However, soon a snag arose in the shortage of first-class accommodation. This gave Andrew Ross the incentive to obtain a site behind the station that overlooked the sea, and there he built the Victoria Hotel. The Highland was supportive. Keen to boost its long-distance travel from Glasgow, it sung the praises of his hotel and compared the cuisine to the Dorchester in London – claims that few could challenge for hyperbole. Certainly there was an abundance of fresh fish, game in season and the service was first rate.

Buoyed up by the success of Ross, the Highland determined to expand its tourist business, seeing themselves in a happy no-lose situation. A little way before the railway reaches Brora they agreed to construct and operate a branch line to Dornoch and, once they commissioned the Station Hotel, they were to focus their holiday publicity there.

Initially, the impact on the Victoria was minimal. Brora continued to thrive, largely due to the impact of the railway. Reflecting this, the Victoria was to change its name to the Station Hotel – possibly aiming to gain from any confusion with Dornoch.

A good barometer of the local economy was the station activity. Coal wagons ran between the local mine and the harbour, and coal dross was sent to hydro-electric stations in Aberdeen. Bricks and drain tiles were despatched to building sites in the north of England; butts of pale malt from the Clynelish distillery were consigned to bonded warehouses in Leith; fish was conveyed by passenger train to Glasgow's fish market and, immediately after auction in the adjacent cattle pens, young lambs, sheep and cattle travelled by goods wagons to Smithfield in London. It mattered not that Hunters Woollen Mills, the largest local employer, used the post office for the despatch of knitting yarn and tweed, since they in turn used the railway's parcel post system. With all this activity, the six station staff were kept busy enough, especially with the arrival of the holidaymakers who packed the special trains during the fortnight of the Glasgow Fair.

Not that Brora's attractions were solely recognised by the Scots. Wealthy Southerners sought it out because, in addition to the golf and fishing, shooting and stalking were within reach. One eminent London surgeon was drawn back year after year on account of the air – the finest he had ever breathed, he would explain, in the course of a long life. Holiday homes were to spring up in Golf Road and they appealed not only to golfers but also to those renting sporting estates in the hills.

Back at the Victoria exotic Continental limousines and sports coupés told of its prosperity. Uniformed chauffeurs polished the two-tone bodywork so fashionable at the time, and the chromium glistened. Guests, too, dressed in style for shooting parties and picnics where crystal and fine Sheffield silverware were unpacked from wicker hampers.

View from the clubhouse *(courtesy of Brora Golf Club)*

Joyce Wethered and her brother Roger at the Worplesdon Foursomes, 1933
(courtesy of Woking Golf Club)

It was a world in which Joyce Wethered and her brother Roger felt totally at ease. Indeed, on their first visit Joyce broke the ladies' record, while Roger broke that for the men. They would travel up from their holiday home in Dornoch to stay with the Duke and Duchess of Sutherland and star in games with members of the aristocracy, including the Marquess of Titchfield, son of the Duke of Portland.

The late Don Macleod recalled how as a youngster he was privileged to caddie for Joyce Wethered. She had arrived with the Duke and his entourage. As they stepped down from a Rolls Royce his stronger colleagues grabbed the most important of the golf bags, thinking they would earn more highly from a gentleman than from a lady. Macleod was left with the lightweight bag. On the rolling fifteenth hole Joyce consulted him on the choice of club for her second shot. He advised the brassie but, doubting this, she conferred with the Duke of Sutherland who suggested a two-iron. When, perfectly struck, it feel short she had the grace to say to Don, 'I suppose you know the course better than the Duke'. He remembers too another golf enthusiast who was won over by Brora: the Bishop of London. Little wonder then that with a clientele like this, the course's reputation soared.

Nearly eighty years on the world has changed much, but in Brora sheep continue to graze alongside cattle and to seek sanctuary in bunkers. At midsummer the midnight competition is still played. So it is that the thread of continuity persists, while Braid's design has survived intact with its successful blend of short, middle-distance, and long holes. Of these it is perhaps the four short holes that give particular pleasure. The sixth is called 'the Witch'. Foreshortened by the mountains the other side of the tracks, it demands a very firm iron to a green on a knoll. The ninth green is tucked down by the shore in full glare of nesting terns and any passing train. The thirteenth is known as 'the Snake'. Here the burn meanders and distracts, and failure to comprehend the wind is punished direly. The last hole too misleads. Though just in range, the temptation is to underclub, so a three here feels rather like a birdie.

Overall there is the joy of open space free of trees that impinge. Nowhere is this more exhilarating than at the seventeenth. The elevated tee encourages a mighty drive. And nothing less will do, for unless one is stymied by a dune or bunkered, the next needs one's all. Then a typically wicked Brora green requires the delicacy of a butterfly to coax the ball into the hole.

All the while on one side are sea views, and on the other purple-clad mountains dotted with cottages that glisten in the sun. Demanding continuous attention of the player are the tortuous burn, the humps and hollows, and the borrows on the speedy greens. It is all immensely special – a legacy from the distinguished trio of John Sutherland, J. H. Taylor and James Braid. Some might regard Brora as a village course, but no other village course can boast such breeding.

Across from Dornoch, on the southern shores of the firth and sheltered by the Struie mountain from westerly winds, is Scotland's oldest royal burgh. This is Tain. It gained the Royal Charter in 1066 when Harold fell at Hastings in trying to repel the Normans.

The town possesses many remarkable buildings. The oldest is the oldest fourteenth-century church which commemorates St Duthus. He was born in

Tain in 1000. Others include a medieval turreted tollbooth, a landmark in the Italianate Parish Church – formerly the Free Church – and a bell tower whose chimes ring out every evening at 8 pm as reminder of the old curfew. Clearly culture has been a friend. As early as 1659 goldsmiths chose to live here, though work bearing the St Duthac hallmark is more likely to date from between 1730 and 1870.

Tain had one advantage over Dornoch. This was the direct link to the south via the Highland Railway. Yet Tain never really established itself as a resort. Probably this is because the sands stretching towards Portmahomack, while marvellous for exercising horses, are less suitable for sunbathing than those of Dornoch or Brora. Still, it has long made a pleasant place for retirement, in large part due to former Bengal banker Alexander MacBean.

When he settled there in the 1880s his one regret was the lack of golf, so he arranged for Old Tom Morris to visit. Eighteen holes were not the rule then, and Old Tom counselled 15. Even this was a little neat for the land which the Town Council made available, and shortly the 15 were reduced to 12. Notwithstanding, golf took a hold, and as soon as further ground was on offer the course was extended to 18 holes.

By 1895 patronage was not just local. The principal trophy was an oriental vase presented by Sir Abdul Ghany, the Nawab of Dacca in East Bengal. He was an old friend of MacBean and the two would have had regular encounters over Dacca's Maidan, where the best line on so many holes is unaccountably an old Hindu temple. The club was now the focal point for the town. Scarcely any young lad of character would have failed to be a caddie or an avid player and some went on to become ambassadors for the game. In 1897 a Tain man carried off the President's Cup in Sri Lanka's Colombo; two years later another introduced golf to Tangiers. Back in Tain these overseas contacts were keenly felt. In 1900, as the spring tournament progressed, news arrived of the Relief of Mafeking. Inside one hour members raised £10 with which they purchased the Baden Powell Cup as a memento and the ninth hole was named Mafeking in remembrance. All the golf holes have names but it is understandable why the naming of this one in particular has long left visitors unfamiliar with the story to scratch their heads in wonderment!

In those days Tain promoted itself through implied physical well-being. There was reference to the healthy climate, admirable drainage and good water, and of course the golf course with its ease of access by rail. Seven trains were to call daily in each direction, and official guides detailed the times, mentioning also that it was seven hours from Edinburgh and Glasgow, fifteen from London, and just an eight-minute walk to the clubhouse (less since it was re-sited from behind the seventeenth green). The Highland Railway was alive to regular repeat business and offered golfers special weekend returns from Inverness at 5s 4d.

Looking across Tain River to the recently rebuilt Edwardian pavilion-style clubhouse
(courtesy of Tain Golf Club)

In support of this a glowing letter was to appear in 1903 in *Golf Illustrated.* Its purpose was to elevate Tain from obscurity.

> The course is much more difficult than at Dornoch. Everybody has heard of the Dornoch Links across the Firth but . . . they are not nearly so sporting, nor are the surroundings nearly so exhilarating.

It went on to liken Tain's ambience to a kind of Scottish Bournemouth – a comparison which fortunately no longer springs to mind. Much more recognisable was reference to the flame-blue of the firth, the pine-covered mountains tipped with snow, and the dry climate!

The natural feel in Tain for golf was so strong that at the end of the Edwardian era when the course was updated no big name was enlisted. Yet the legacy is as intriguing as any. Not one hole travels in the same direction as another so, when the wind gusts, players become bemused before being confounded by the fine but racy greens. Gorse and heather prey, a burn intrudes and the faces of bunkers, while fair, are severe, particularly under the Alps at the eleventh.

It was Peter Alliss, the former Ryder Cup player who succeeded Henry

Longhurst as the most understanding of television's commentators, who summed up the third hole as Scotland's best par 4 in the north. Other candidates could well be the third at Moray, the ninth at Golspie, the eleventh at Royal Dornoch, or the twelfth at Nairn. Be that as it may, none of these distinguished holes can compete with the northerly spectacle which quite takes the breath away as one stands on the high point of Tain's wickedly sloping third green. To the west and below the imposing Struie Hill there nestles the stately town flanked by Glenmorangie's distillery. Behind and to its right distant mountains tower above Skibo. Then in glorious array lie the Sutherland hills furnishing a backcloth to the Dornoch Firth and the cathedral town from which the firth takes its name. In winter, when their snow-capped peaks glisten in the morning sun, this is especially enchanting. Given decent light at any time of the year, it is something worth crossing the Atlantic to experience, which, strangely, very few do.

Following the course to the end, the burn returns with a vengeance surrounding the sixteenth green on three sides. Then at the 215-yard seventeenth one has to cross it twice where it lies in wait to consign a push or slice to a watery grave, and metes out similar punishment at the last as well. From start to finish Tain tantalises and its greens mesmerise. Every hole is distinctive and in one way or another is distinguished as well. Small wonder then that connoisseurs and holiday golfers are captivated by a course that is maintained quite beautifully by green-keepers who also play the game wonderfully well. It is a major find never deserving of obscurity, which many consider the most entertaining of all that the north of Scotland can offer.

In short, since there has been a bridge across the firth a mile or two from Skibo, Dornoch has a real rival on its hands in Tain for the title of the perfect centre. In any club handicapper's portfolio it has to be in the first division. One thing is certain, Alexander MacBean would be immensely proud of the course should he revisit today. How he must have preferred Tain to Dacca!

Golf Among the Mountains

The traditional Scottish courses of world repute tended to be seaside links. Here is golf at its most natural where breezes vary as the tide turns and dexterity is called upon to play its part in defeating the elements. The Open Championship has only ever been played on a links, and this is no accident for no one can aspire to be the titleholder unless he can master the unexpected – the prerequisite of any good links course.

Golf among the mountains requires comparable attributes. Great length may not be one but versatility and the art of judging distance most certainly are. More than anywhere else in Britain, it is Scotland that offers the golfer excitement among the mountains.

Within the spectacular setting of the Cairngorms are four courses which used to be served by the main railway line to the north. Two still are; the third, Boat of Garten, is privy to steam trains in the summer season; but the fourth, Grantown, is regrettably deprived. It retains as sole reminder of its railway heritage a superb castellated bridge over the Forres road.

The most southerly of the four is Newtonmore, known for its high proportion of left-handers who were formerly shinty players. This is a gentle course that perambulates the plain between the railway and the River Spey. Bordering it a few comely villas, which date from the last quarter of the nineteenth century, have commanding views. The visitor looks up to them in envy.

Though the terrain is flattish one ought not to underestimate the golf, as the layout is an early James Braid design of 1893. He had a feel for the picturesque and sited the greens well. Their quality is excellent and locally they are considered second only to Nairn. It is a most successful small town course with the added bonus of one exceptional hole in the middle where the Spey terrorises throughout. Even when it eludes the eye, the rush of waters over varnished pebbles conveys its presence. Their cadence contrasts with birdsong overhead and the rumble of an occasional train.

Next stop is Kingussie. Quite unlike Newtonmore no fairway is visible from the railway: built in 1891 the course is a mile or more up the mountain. Over the first three holes woodland awaits a hook. Then the fifth demands a full frontal assault on the mountain Carn an Fhreiceadain. The next two holes cling to its side from where there are views even more glorious than at Gleneagles.

Excitement continues as two short holes follow in succession. The first is over a boulder-laden precipice harbouring scores of trees and a mountain stream. The second is uphill and blind. Then it is on to open country with drives from elevated tees (Henry Cotton's favourite), shots silhouetted against far off crags, serious par fours, and two more devious back-to-back short holes. The moment the pretty little clubhouse is in sight, the burn reappears – hostile to both hooker and the brazen. This is holiday golf *par excellence*, thanks to the enlightened design of Harry Vardon and Sandy Herd, Open Champion in 1902 and the man who did most to popularise the Haskell ball.

Boat of Garten's railway is no longer part of the main network. The line used to run over the Dava moor to Forres when it provided the principal route to the Moray Firth, but at the time of the Beeching axe the connection at Aviemore was severed. All that remains is the steam shuttle between Aviemore and Boat of Garten which is operated by the Strathspey Railway, though hopes run high that this will be extended once again to Grantown. Certainly a new rail overbridge outside the clubhouse entrance augurs well for this.

Though James Braid is credited with Boat of Garten's design, he was not the instigator. Uniquely, it started life as a six-hole divertissement built by local railway workers with the help of a handful of volunteers. Only the first hole betrays these humble origins. From the second onwards beauty assails the senses. Holes are framed by silver birch and evergreen, gullies beckon, heather intrudes, and smallish greens on pinnacles tantalise.

Boat is best played with a balata ball on a cheerful day when it is damp underfoot. Should sunlight filter through the trees, the views of the Cairngorms captivate and it is scarcely surprising some tees have seats that face the view rather than the hole. Almost more than any other holiday course in Scotland, it has acquired a loyal fan club the world over. For them 'Boat is best'.

The fourth of these Cairngorm courses is Grantown which enjoys a delightful situation beside dense woodland masking the Spey. Beyond, the hills of Cromdale form a striking backcloth. Their power is softened through shades of purple and green, though even towards the end of May one can still expect to see them wear a snowy mantle. This is a wonderful time of year when the air is sharp and the light is bright.

Grantown shares with Golspie the unusual feature of three distinct sections, each of six holes. Firstly, there is parkland worthy of a Duke's deer herd. Then there is heathland with holes of great beauty and imagination to test the expertise of the most highly skilled. The final six own to a moorland character. They tease and confound. Again, the course pedigree is outstanding with Willie Park and James Braid being responsible.

Further north, beyond Inverness but below Ben Wyvis, Strathpeffer Spa is as elegant a Victorian town as was ever created. Its setting and architecture conjure thoughts of an idealised American pioneer station. Behind timber balustrades, spacious gabled houses boast broad balconies carefully angled to offer sequestered sunshine and mountain views.

Strathpeffer should have been the foremost station on the Dingwall to Skye Railway. When that eminent engineer, Joseph Mitchell, surveyed the route in 1863, his recommendation was that the line pass through it and on to Contin for the spa was the principal town of any size west of Dingwall, earning a reputation as 'the Harrogate of the north'. Mitchell reckoned that if the line were to be built economically, and to cater both for tourism and the west coast

The *Strathy* arriving at Strathpeffer Spa from Dingwall
(*courtesy of Locomotive & General Railways Photographs*)

fishing, it could more than earn its keep. After all, he maintained, the scenery was the finest in the Highlands and the fish stocks were inexhaustible!

However it was not to be. A number of local landowners were obstructive, of whom Sir William Mackenzie of Coul was principal. The line would have passed through four miles of his estate and within a quarter of a mile of his residence. Sensing he held the major cards, he insisted on a lengthy tunnel with its arches grassed over and embankments manicured. Then he demanded free rail for himself and his heirs. The tunnel happened to be impractical as well as unnecessary for no trains would have been in sight from the great house. Disappointed and somewhat at a loss, the Dingwall and Skye directors would have no truck with him. When Mitchell took to writing his memoirs as an elderly man, he felt this had been a mistake and that they should have endeavoured to reach an accommodation.

Bypassing Strathpeffer saved only £18,000. Instead the route went north and a little station built at Achterneed was christened 'Strathpeffer' regardless of the fact that it was not particularly convenient. Only when Sir William died could the town be linked into the rail system. Once the crops had been gathered in a branch line was constructed. It duly opened on 3 June, in time for the summer season of 1885, at which time the station on the main line was renamed Achterneed.

By now the Dingwall & Skye Railway had succumbed to the Highland Railway. Fully aware of Strathpeffer's potential, the Highland chose to concentrate on the branch rather than the main line to the Kyle of Lochalsh, whose lack of success had contributed to the smaller company's demise. The line was also beginning to suffer competition from steamers to Skye and Lewis. With the spa becoming a terminus and the tail, so to speak, now wagging the dog, the Strathpeffer service merited promotion.

Since taking the waters was very much in fashion, the town opted to focus on the affluent and the hypochondriac, and followed Nairn's example in deciding to create a golf course. The leading Scottish player of the day, Willie Park, was invited to design it. Next year he was to win the Open for the second time. Charismatic and persuasive, he was not then the noted designer he was to become. He cut his teeth on this one rather, achieving a somewhat rudimentary nine-hole layout among Ulladale's sloping fields that encircled the curling pond.

Needless to say the locals were thrilled, and in June 1888 it was opened in great style. The *Ross-shire Journal* reported that Miss Lawson of Leys Castle 'struck off a very nice shot, which went over the brow of the hill . . . amidst the cheer of the onlookers'. Competitors came from far and wide: they represented clubs as exclusive as Royal Aberdeen, Bruntsfield, Elie and Prestwick. A Hungarian band played in the background; the weather was delightful; and wine and cake was served. This was just the send-off the little course needed;

golf could now complement the spa's other attractions.

All seemed well enough but with the passage of time the Highland Railway became complacent, profiting from passengers and treating Strathpeffer as it would a milch cow. By the turn of the century passengers were still changing at Dingwall for the two-mile shuttle. Those less able objected, hoteliers complained and even Highland's Chairman admitted that while the antiquated rolling stock might be adequate for Hottentots, it was not good enough for carrying ordinary Christian Scotsmen. Adding to the pressure from shareholders with a vested interest in the spa's prosperity, there was a clamour for through carriages labelled 'London-Strathpeffer'. Nothing less would do!

By 1903 the original croft clubhouse needed replacing. At a cost of £400 a new one was erected – a charming pavilion with a veranda running its entire width. Four years later the course was upgraded to 18 holes, and what had been a rather insignificant first hole was extended to provide a massive drop unsuitable for anyone subject to vertigo. Thereafter with one exception, until the last hole that runs equally sharply downhill, the climb is gradual and ever upward.

To celebrate the enlarged course an exhibition match was held one lovely day in September. The participants were Arnaud Massy, the Basque who was current Open Champion, and that Yorkshire stalwart, Sandy Herd. The two were on tour and a couple of days earlier Massy had trounced Herd at Spey Bay. At Strathpeffer he was to admit defeat by 5/4 in the morning and by 2/1 in the afternoon. Herd's score of 66 was an eye-opener. Not surprisingly he said, 'I never saw anything prettier.' Massy held his counsel but later wrote graciously from the Versailles club of La Boulie to say he had found it 'magnifique'.

Willie Park's layout of nine holes had now been transformed along the lines suggested by Harold Hilton and Horace Hutchinson for, wherever it was practical, holes were grouped in threes to facilitate cutting across. The views were now even more spectacular compounded as they are with a tenth tee which is 'out of this world'.

There was no question about it; golf was adding lustre to the spa's attractions. So the Highland Railway took the decision to involve itself further and to promote Strathpeffer more actively. They purchased a 16hp Albion motorcar, had it specially painted and decorated with slogans and sent it on tour to the north of England. While preparations were in hand, those local businessmen who had been upbraiding the Highland Railway as doing far too little for the town were invited to put their hands in their pockets and support it financially. Other than the proprietors of the spa waters, these voluble critics feigned deafness. So the Highland was to bear the brunt of the expenditure as citizens of Oldham, Rochdale, Newcastle, and a dozen other northern towns learnt of Strathpeffer's virtues. Alas journalists were amused rather than impressed: one called the resort 'the Sanatorium of the British Isles'.

In conjunction with this safari, and to appeal to Londoners, a through carriage ran to Strathpeffer, firstly from King's Cross, then from Euston. The Chairman added his two ha'pennyworth, claiming archly that people who had foolishly crossed the channel in quest of a cure could now find one which 'worked just as well very much nearer home'.

The Highland Railway had long appreciated that the holiday trade produced the icing on the cake. Even though the hotel at Brora was owned by a local entrepreneur, they enjoyed good business to the resort. Meanwhile, at Dornoch they profited from both the rail receipts and their own magnificent Station Hotel. What could be more sensible then than to repeat the process at Strathpeffer!

So they splashed out £50,000 on a luxury hotel nearly half as big again at 90 bedrooms, and endowed it with their own name, The Highland. It had a commanding aspect over the Spa, was near the bowling green and a lane ran from it to the golf course. Gables and towers contrived to give it the appearance of a Medoc chateau and inside wood panelling adorned each of the immense public rooms. Confidence was writ large and in 1911, with no expense spared, it was opened.

The invited guests arrived by train from as far away as London. On board, and once at the hotel, they were treated like royalty. So that they could fully grasp the splendour of the scenery, an exhibition match presided over by Lord Lovat was staged. Sandy Herd was called upon again and he and J. H. Taylor did battle in partnership with the top two local amateurs.

Notwithstanding such an auspicious and costly launch, the hotel never really justified itself. Three years later the country was at war and the Victorian love of 'the waters' was on the wane. When in 1923 the Highland Railway company was absorbed into the London Midland & Scottish Railway, the new hierarchy decided that the expense in keeping the hotel open out of season was not warranted and it was closed between the end of September and mid May each year. By 1929 even the spa company was in difficulties. Patronage was dwindling and it owed £3,000.

After World War II the LMS put the hotel on the market, then had to wait twelve years for a buyer.

If the judgement of those Highland Railway directors was clouded by exuberance in this instance, they were certainly not lacking the will to cultivate connections. With a series of poster advertisements promoting 'The Picturesque Line of the Empire' their publicity had been imaginative if not poetic. Scotsmen abroad were exhorted to visit Strathpeffer for a well-earned rest when they next were home. Perhaps the best known was 'The Doctor Prescribes' in which a prosperous physician is wagging a finger in admonishment at the reader:

Sick? Nonsense, man! You are city sick, that's all. Go to the Highlands and take your golf clubs with you.

He went so far as to prescribe even the route: via Perth. In another, 'The Minister Muses' a clergyman sits thoughtfully at his desk, 'longing for a sight of Strathpeffer'. Yet others regularly featured an angler and a caddie.

In addition to these posters, worked editorials were to appear in the middle-class newspapers. They commented on the special express trains that Strathpeffer enjoyed, they listed the current most notable visitors, extolled the quality of the fishing and golf and, of course, the all-inclusive facilities of the Highland Hotel.

Even more sophisticated was the 64-page green leatherette book that the railway company issued free to doctors entitled *A Medical Guide to Strathpeffer*. This listed all the baths, the waters and the type of treatment on offer. As the waters were particularly heavy in sulphur and tasted filthy, the emphasis was on their benefits to a whole range of problems. A subtle approach was one recommended by the local Dr Manson. He explained how the waters tended to prevent the onset of uric acid, known to be the deadly enemy of the rich and bons vivants.

Supporting this propaganda the Highland made a concerted effort to enhance their passenger services. On a Tuesday they ran a special through train from Aviemore known as the Strathpeffer Spa Express. This connected with trains from Edinburgh, Glasgow and Dundee, and saved time by cutting out Inverness. All-inclusive tickets for the train and hotel were available at London North West Railway stations. London had its own through sleeper services which ran via Inverness. Local branding took place too, earning goodwill and affection: the little train from Dingwall that plied the branch was known as 'The Strathy', while its tank engine and carriages were proudly printed 'Strathpeffer'.

For a time this had all seemed to entice visitors northward. But when fashion changed there was no going back. Critics even pointed an incriminating finger at the sulphurous Highland waters, blaming it for outbreaks of cholera. In their place pure water was extolled. For all its loveliness the golf course had only ever been built as an adjunct to the spa and a place to relax. With so many major relatively level seaside links less than an hour away, it scarcely justified being the principal stopover for a golfing holiday. In 1946, as if to reinforce their commercial decision to offer the Highland Hotel for sale, the LMS withdrew passenger services. Five years later it closed the branch down for freight as well.

The town now resembles a museum. The station is one. Echoes of Hungarian music may have long since been dispelled, but the golf course

Local pride in the local train *(courtesy of David Thomas)*

continues as the happiest of hunting grounds in surroundings which can justly be described as idyllic, well away from any house or garden. Nowhere does the click and crack of the golf ball echo more pleasurably, although judgement of distance is best left to the eye as a card or distance marker will surely confuse.

Mountain golf is a world apart from links golf or the inland game. There is the thrill of a descending blow on lavish but forgiving turf, and amazement when the pace of the green is correctly gauged on gradients cruel beyond compare. If nerves can be held in check the patient player will be both relieved and exhilarated. But then that will also have been the effect on those who sought the succour of the Spa waters.

The Moray Firth Riviera

Part I

It was due to the benign climate and superb quality of its farming land that the Scottish aristocracy favoured the Moray Firth. Even now the ancient castles of Cawdor, Brodie and Darnaway remain family houses in part and many of the old landed estates are intact, though some have been diminished as inheritances were gambled away in the fleshpots of London or Monte Carlo.

The area has much to offer. The riches of the plain support grain, cattle and pigs. On the hills forests burgeon. Its lakes contain brown trout, famous salmon rivers attract the angler, and within the call of the Spey lie many of Scotland's most noted distilleries.

However it was sea-fishing that provided the livelihoods for the coastal towns and villages. By the end of the nineteenth century the area was humming – fishing was never more thriving and the railway too was buoyant. Lord Cockburn's remarks of 50 years earlier still rang true:

> Those who are born to railroads . . . can scarcely be made to understand how we, of the previous age, got on.

It was the era of railway fever. In 1845, 620 railway companies were registered. In aggregate they commanded a capital of £563 million, a huge sum at the time. Even tiny companies whose ambitions were limited were formed, so eager were the public to clamber aboard.

As ever timing was of the essence. Four years earlier in 1841 Joseph Mitchell had conceived of a railway between Elgin and the little port of Lossiemouth. He surveyed the route, found a contractor and the following year set up a company with an Elgin solicitor. But the concept was just in advance of the public's appetite for such a venture, and others were to follow where he had led. A few years made all the difference – though the capital required for a railway from Inverness to Aberdeen was only £300,000, the promoters actually raised £2 million.

Then came the Great Railway Crash of 1847. Stocks became unsaleable. Investors who held partly paid shares and faced a call defaulted in droves.

Not everyone of course, even at the outset, was in favour of railways. Lady Seafield echoed the Duke of Wellington in considering they brought together such an objectionable variety of people. Captain Grant, her factor on the Seafield estates at Strathspey, shared her antagonism. One concern of his was that steam trains would frighten away the grouse. Another was, that with the railways certain to be the dominant freight carrier, what would become of the 40 floaters who carried on the tradition of their forebears in floating timber down the Spey from the pine forests of Abernethy and Dulnain to the port of Garmouth for shipping.

It was not until 1858 that the railway from Inverness to Aberdeen was finally completed. With the economic climate having been so volatile, the process had not been without its share of sagas. The driving force to link the two together and to open up the Moray Firth area was the Great North of Scotland Railway. In 1846 they had obtained the power and the capital to construct the line though in the aftermath of the Crash backers had pulled out and they were strapped for cash. Accordingly, they curtailed their ambitions and built the line from Aberdeen only as far as Huntly. Extending it west to Keith came later.

Meanwhile, they were pre-empted at the Inverness end by a local initiative with backing from Nairn. The line that linked these two towns opened in November 1855. Progress had been rapid. Even Lady Seafield was caught up in all the enthusiasm, being persuaded to cut the first sod in September 1854. The cost of reaching Nairn was £85,000, but so forward-thinking was the contractor that his firm accepted shares worth £20,000 instead of cash! To extend the line on to Elgin required the support of two major landowners. These were the Earls of Seafield and Fife; both were persuaded and subscribed £30,000 each.

When the Great Northern felt sufficiently confident to edge westwards, the logistics of completing the line between Aberdeen and Inverness became ever more complex. The sticking point was the high cost of bridging the Spey. As the Inverness & Nairn Railway terminated at Elgin its directors declined to get involved.

The problem was resolved through the good offices of Joseph Mitchell. This outstanding surveyor had a plan which would save the GNOSR £50,000 and with this more tempting offer they invited the Highland Railway to participate. The Highland line ran from Aviemore through Grantown to Elgin. Well aware that this would be the main artery between the Moray Firth and the south, they agreed to build the missing link between Elgin and Keith on behalf of the

Elegance and style at Nairn station, 1913
(courtesy of Locomotive & General Railways Photographs)

GNOSR and to share the viaduct costs 50:50. Mitchell's plan was to change the gradient of a two-and-a-half-mile stretch of track on the east of the Spey from 1:60 to 1:100 and so lower the height of the viaduct by 30 feet. Retaining £10,000 of the saving in costs, the GNOSR now used the spare £40,000 to fund the Highland's charges for the extension to Keith.

In 1858 the Nairn to Keith line opened. But not all the problems had been resolved. Against Mitchell's advice the directors had pushed on without first obtaining Board of Trade sanction. It was now found that the scaffolding supporting the bridge was sinking due to the vibration caused every time a locomotive and train passed over. Consequently, while reparations were proceeding passengers had to get out and walk along the adjoining suspension bridge. Once the empty train had been pushed across without its locomotive, they could climb back in. On the far side a fresh locomotive was on hand which conveyed them on to Keith.

With the two main cities in the north finally rail connected, it was only a matter of time before a criss-cross network was developed, giving most little towns their own station. The Moray Firth area was now readily accessible and great change was not long in coming.

Nairn was a particular beneficiary. This was due largely to the efforts of Dr John Grigor. He was an indefatigable publicist who promoted it the year round. He commended the climate as dry, bracing, and free from mist and fog; and he advocated its sea as suitable bathing for convalescents. As a result, the town developed into a place for retirement and a winter resort. Comparison was made with Italy's San Remo, and the claim put forward that in February it was often warmer in Nairn! Colonels and ex-colonials settled gladly. Large stone houses of quality were built in the residential area of the west end. Soon Nairn established for itself a special reputation, becoming known as the Brighton of the North, so much so that by 1880 over half the visitors arriving by rail came from London or the south.

Along with Nairn other coastal towns set their sights on tourism in a purposeful diversification. Bowling greens and golf courses were to appear, but neither sport was exactly new. Dornoch had known golf since the sixteenth century as had Morayshire, for in 1596 a goldsmith from Elgin was fined and censured for 'playing at the boulis and golff, upoun Sondaye in the tyme of the sermon'.

In Nairn it was the fishermen who had played 'bools', rolling heavy iron balls on the Links – not a golf course, but a large grassy area which was once the location of the public baths and today is home to a scenic cricket pitch that overlooks the Moray Firth and Black Isle.

In contrast, the gentry took to golf. In 1887, some thirty years after the railways had ushered in an era of prosperity, a number of them were determined that Nairn have a club. A committee of 15 was formed to include Robert Finlay, the local Member of Parliament and a notable QC; a London barrister (who went on to become a founder member of Woking and Lord Chief Justice); three solicitors; two doctors; a General and a Colonel.

Well-to-do they may have been, but they were careful too: £36 was paid to Andrew Simpson, the greenkeeper at Aberdeen, to design the course – less than half the salary of the first greenkeeper, a Musselburgh man who within three years was fired for insolence.

Nevertheless, golf at Nairn made immediate appeal and members of the Inverness club were envious of its aspect and quality of turf. For a bulk subscription they sought playing rights but were rebuffed. Nairn had no wish to become a satellite to their larger neighbour.

Like that early greenkeeper, Simpson's design did not last long either. In 1890 Old Tom Morris extended the course towards the fishing village of Delnies. Then in 1919 Ben Sayers of North Berwick created new holes on the

Earl of Cawdor's land going as far as the old Ice House. Barrels of beef and lamb were stored here, where ice hewn from lochs in the hills behind Geddes and Cawdor, and carted along the narrow lanes, acted as a preservative.

In 1909 James Braid had updated Old Tom's layout and he gave his services again in 1921. It was then he reported:

> The putting greens were always the outstanding feature . . . and still fully maintain their excellence. The texture of the turf and the character of the greens are unrivalled.

He also made a comment which is equally apt and just as relevant today:

> I find I get less tired on this than on any other of its kind. I think the reason is that the sub-soil is of very light sand, with a peculiarly springy quality of turf on top.

Meanwhile, fishermen and tradesmen were gifted land at the other end of town by Sir Alexander Dunbar so they, too, could enjoy golf. Nine holes were built

Nairn's homely clubhouse, demolished 1989 *(author's photograph)*

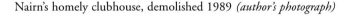

initially. Nairn Dunbar golf course is rightly proud of its roots and does not cloak its fierce wish to rival the reputation of the Nairn. A new clubhouse, and three new holes backing on to the bird sanctuary bordering East Beach, which runs into the Culbin Sands, are handsome testimony to Dunbar's status as a championship course. As such, it does not suffer from the 'nine out – nine back' syndrome that is all too common on Scottish seaside links. It affords immense pleasure and is very well regarded even though, or possibly because, it is long, difficult and has a number of small landing areas.

Its quality is such that Nairn may well be the only town of its size in Great Britain – around 10,000 inhabitants or less – to have two such courses of high calibre literally on its doorstep.

The Nairn, too, had a benefactor in Robert Finlay. As a Queen's Counsel he successfully defended the directors of the White Star line against a charge of callous conduct towards those below decks when the Titanic struck an iceberg and sank. Later he rose to become Solicitor General, Attorney General and, finally, Lord Chancellor. Hugely distinguished he was also generous. He paid for two-thirds of Simpson's bill, met the cost of extending the clubhouse and

Ben Alisky – a Ben class loco at Nairn station. Could the hamper be for Newton House? *(courtesy of Locomotive & General Railways Photographs)*

donated a silver cup to be played for among the clubs in his constituency. Owner of the imposing Newton House, he leased sufficient of its ample grounds to enable the club to build a nine-hole ladies course.

It was through Finlay that Nairn acquired cachet among the influential in London. He was elevated to Viscount and his bountiful hospitality became legendary. House guests numbered parliamentary colleagues, one of whom naturally was golf's foremost addict, the Prime Minister of the time, A. J. Balfour. When Parliament entered recess, Finlay's arrival back at Nairn station would provoke a remarkable spectacle. Accompanied by at least fifteen servants, he was met by a cavalcade of carriages and carts. After the luggage had been carefully stowed the convoy proceeded in stately fashion to Newton House. There his flag was hoist and his personal caddie remained at the ready. The holidays literally turned into one long golfing party.

Finlay was not the only host of munificence. The club president was the Earl of Cawdor who in 1905 was first Lord of the Admiralty. Among those lured by the atmosphere and the golf were Field Marshal Earl Haig; Lt Col McNeile, rather better known as 'Sapper' and author of the Bulldog Drummond tales; Ramsay MacDonald, later to be Prime Minister; and the Prince of Wales. After the Second World War prominent visitors included Charlie Chaplin and Harold Macmillan though they sought peace rather than golf.

Nairn inspires a deep-seated loyalty. The most eminent of those who had the good fortune to learn their game there was David Blair. A major in the Fifth Seaforth Highlanders, a director of the Distillers Company in charge of Black & White whisky, an old Harrovian and the doyen of their Halford Hewitt team, he was also the 1953 Scottish Amateur Champion and was twice a Walker Cup player. For years he entered tournaments from Nairn even though he was to play more at St Andrews, Troon and Muirfield. For Blair, the links where he had honed his skills under his father's tutelage long had a claim to his heart and sense of challenge.

In 1929, when Blair was still a lad, Viscount Finlay died. House parties lost their glossiness and to some extent Nairn opted for a back seat. Other than a few ladies tournaments, some Northern Opens and the 1954 Scottish Amateur Championship, the club staged relatively little of national significance. Not until 1959 did word of Nairn's subtleties and beauty begin to circulate again. This was the occasion of Britain's first Golf Week, a concept fostered by two go-getting members and the Nairn Development Association with the Golf View Hotel very much to the fore. Henry Cotton was persuaded to be the master coach. The next year he came again. Then he was succeeded by Dai Rees, captain of the Ryder Cup in 1957, and Max Faulkner, who was the second Englishman of his day ever to win the Open. His year of glory was 1951.

The days of old money and whisky-swilling Colonels were now rooted in the past. Twice more the Scottish Amateur was held, in 1964, and in 1987 when Colin Montgomerie won. The Royal & Ancient was now taking notice and chose Nairn to host the Vagliano Trophy, for which the leading ladies of Britain and Europe still compete.

Then in 1994, in its 110th year, the Amateur Championship came to Nairn for the first time. Viscount Whitelaw took a week's holiday to watch. He had been brought up in the town as a small boy. A former deputy Prime Minister to Margaret Thatcher, and club president, he was joined by Charlie Yates. This spry octogenarian had played top and triumphed in his single for the USA in the 1938 Walker Cup at St Andrews, which Great Britain and Ireland won against expectations. Still a stalwart of the Augusta club where the Masters is held every April, he knew Nairn well for he was an honorary life member.

Neither was surprised at the unstinting approval it earned. After all, where else could one find a links with sea views from every hole, greens so superlative they still lived up to James Braid's description of more than 70 years earlier and, in addition, a clubhouse permitting an unparalleled vista of the course, the Moray Firth, the Black Isle and the snow-capped mountain range alongside Ben Wyvis.

The course itself is endowed with the qualities of a chameleon. Off the front tees the long handicapper can enjoy himself. From the white tees it presents a major test, stern yet feasible. From the blue tees, of which several were constructed specially for the Amateur, the examination is of the strictest and, for most, an ordeal. It is Nairn's genius that it can appeal to all, though no one should be deluded by the amiability of its start with the softness of the Five Sisters of Kintail on the distant blue horizon.

The first seven holes flank the firth. In places the waters are so close that at high tide one could cast in a broken tee. Certainly those with a propensity to slice are well advised to consult a tide chart before agreeing a starting time! At the third, the course first shows its real mettle. A dog-leg, it edges away from the shore past a greenkeeper's shed. This antique relic from the club's early days is lovingly maintained and poses a formidable hazard to the hooker. The drive is tight and only a second shot of distinction suffices if the ball is to lodge on the green. Similar attributes apply at the fifth where the beach nudges into play.

In-between, the short fourth perplexes for it runs counter to the general direction of the outward half to face the Culbin Sands and Lossiemouth. Two steep bunkers, a long-waisted green and the sea breakwater, fight for the privilege of attracting a ball at the mercy of the wind.

Then come heather and gorse and the long trek out to the Ice House broken only by Delnies, the eighth hole. That, too, faces east. From the only semi-blind tee shot a short pitch necessitates the subtlety of a cat after a mole, and the better the drive the more devilish is the approach. In the reverse direction the

Nairn's seventeenth hole. Original painting by Alex J. Webster
(courtesy of the artist)

ninth is nearly as awkward. The drive is tight, and the fairway a strain to reach off the blue tee. Two pot bunkers await the fade while anywhere short of the gorse on the left gives rise to a fiendish pitch. Four bunkers guard a green that slopes from left to right. Another short par 4 it may be, but a birdie chance is seldom realised.

Homeward bound one has the assistance of the prevailing westerly wind. Regardless, the twelfth fascinates for it always demands two shots of impeccable quality. Next comes an equally fearsome test on tackling three holes which run at right angles to the main stream of play. First one climbs up Nairn's only hill to the thirteenth green and fourteenth tee. From here the view is spell-binding. It justifies the time and patience of artist and photographer; and it is not unknown for visitors to linger for hours in awe. Acres of woodland isolate both holes embellishing the gorse and endless clumps of heather. Heading towards the firth one discerns the undulations of the fifteenth fairway. On the far side is the Black Isle in hues of an antique counterpane, and lorded over by the mountains of Easter Ross. Above all, it is the myriad shades of blue which startle. Sometimes the sea is the deepest navy; at others it is a pale shimmering cerulean interspersed with a mirror flat silver, and enlivened only by a tiny fishing smack or simple craft as it skims the surface in search of dolphins.

The fifteenth is rather special. The drive is between two magnificent pines set dauntingly close to the tee. Negotiating these, it must still clear heather and scrub and a gaping fairway bunker on soaring towards the sea and the mountains beyond. The green is wide but shallow. Guarding it is a swale, and a pocket-sized sand trap that engulfs any ball caught by the prevailing wind. The approach calls for infinite finesse. This is the third of three short par fours. Old-fashioned they may be but they offer an exquisite reminder of Nairn's individuality.

It is no surprise, therefore, that this course has pride of place in the north of Scotland, well deserving the honour of being the battleground for the 1999 Walker Cup, which Great Britain and Ireland won with a brilliance probably unequalled in the annals of the Amateur game.

Part II

Delight at golf along the Moray Firth is not confined to Nairn. To the east, Hopeman has a rugged cliff-top course whose several majestic views of the firth excel all others. Originally only nine holes, its current 18 offer village golf at its most enjoyable. The most memorable hole is the spectacular short twelfth. From the high point of the course one strikes into a vast bowl. Here is a world of intrepid bracken in which the green is an oasis; to the right a swirling sea and hostile shore are unforgiving. Any ball whipped by a stiff south-westerly must be instantly forgotten, but then any form of mishit will signify a lost ball. Nothing could be more intimidating.

Hopeman used to be the terminus for a little spur, built in 1892 and accessed from the Burghead branch line. The station was tucked in behind the dunes at the foot of the High Street and within a stone's throw of the harbour and sandy bay. The scene is of the prettiest and must have graced many a postcard. In the Beeching era the spur was a casualty of the passenger-network cut-backs, regardless that part of the original branch continued to cater for two large maltings. Its loss mainly inconvenienced film directors who made use of its little-known and picturesque situation.

However, the old Highland railway carriage which had acted as Hopeman's station found another lease of life. This was divided into two and six dray horses hauled each to a knoll beside the first tee. The two halves were then re-joined and for over ten years they served as the golf clubhouse.

Another little place long deprived of its railway is Cullen. For five centuries it was a fishing village famous for haddock, and it gave its name to Cullen Skink – a haddock-based fish soup. Cullen used to be dry. In consequence an enterprising Scot established the Bay Hotel just outside the boundary. Here, away from prying eyes, thirsty fishermen resorted to a dram to ease their harsh existence.

Transcending this soft and charming town is the railway viaduct of 1884. It looks to be an extraordinary extravagance and indeed it was, for the Earl of Seafield who lived at the 386-roomed Cullen House, and was on the Board of the Highland Railway, insisted that the GNOSR keep well clear of his grounds. This unco-operative competitor added hugely to the cost of construction of the railway. The Earl, however, was recalcitrant. He refused to use the local Cullen station and insisted that his family and house guests travel only via the Highland Railway. That meant taking a gig to Rathven, a few miles towards Buckie, from where the branch line train ran to Keith giving connections into the main line.

Cullen's golf course preceded the railway by five years. Initially it was just nine holes. Then in 1904 it was expanded to 18 with the help of Old Tom Morris. It was a far-sighted move that recognised the little fishing port had seen its best days, and that any boost to the economy of the town would be dependent on tourism. The club was bold. Casting its net wide it advertised itself as six hours by train from Glasgow, and just 14 hours from London.

The course lies on two plateaux. One is at sea level while the other is atop rose-coloured sandstone cliffs which overlook the two miles of Cullen Bay, ranging from Scar Nose by Portknockie to Logie Head. The lower holes shelter within this backcloth and weave around rocky outcrops of the same sandstone. Rather grandly, if quite justified, these are known as the 'Three Kings'. They form intrinsic obstacles in giving rise to blind shots on to greens that are sited with a certain sense of mischief.

Before them another kind of challenge has to be surmounted – quite literally. The second tee is elevated well above the first green. Ahead lies an overgrown chasm and crossing this necessitates a near vertical climb. No green is visible; neither is the flagstick. The only guide is that at the top of the escarpment there is a tall, black-and-white barber's pole, rather than the traditional red and white. Beyond is the sky. Just that – no mountain; not even a tree. Simply a case of heavens above!

One needs progress slowly. Even then the breath is taken away, for on reaching the green virtually all the course unfolds, with a further five holes on the upper plateau and the remainder meandering below. Out in the bay the light shimmers in patches of silver and blue, or an iridescent indigo, lilac and orange, while tumbling on to the shore come waves as wide as giant carpets. This is the view to have mesmerised passengers as their train emerged from the cutting alongside the second and third; a rich experience denied to the Earl's house guests unfamiliar with golf!

At the blind fourth another shot into the sky is required, necessitating positive thinking and perfect timing if the wind is not to play havoc. Then three holes later recklessness challenges caution as one descends to the plateau below.

Should one skirt the escarpment or play meekly at an angle approaching 45 degrees? Fortune may favour the brave with a drive floating down on the green 230 yards away. On the other hand, the punishment for failure will bring a rueful smile to the meek, for there is rough in the manner of Harlech to swallow up the ball.

Overall the course is not long, but it is entertaining and judgement of distance exercises the mind continually. A visitor will be well advised to negotiate hard before agreeing terms with a local player.

Not far to the west lies Buckie. This was the largest of the Moray fishing ports and remains a fish market of importance. Along cliffs on either side of the town golfers have a treat: to the west is Buckpool and to the east, Strathlene. Built in 1877 the Strathlene course pre-dates Nairn by a decade. Within seven years it was bordered by the Highland line which ran from Keith to Portessie, whose station was shared with the GNOSR. From there the line ran through Cullen to the ancient town of Portsoy where it terminated at the harbour built in 1693. Herring, grain, timber and marble were its main cargo though these gradually declined as the railway tended to siphon business off rather than acting as a catalyst to growth.

When the Highland station closed in 1939, the building was moved a little way from Portessie and Strathlene's members used it happily as a clubhouse until 1973. It was a handsome edifice with a veranda and had 'Strathlene Golf Course' painted in bold white letters on the roof. Its replacement has none of the original's charm or style; built after the fashion of the time it resembles a thick wedge of cheese.

Somehow a sense of déjà vu permeates the course. Behind the sixteenth hole an unkempt embankment and stone wall mask the former track bed. Now with no good folk peering out of carriage windows to view one's faltering efforts in mastering a dog-leg, or pitching to a green that might well have been designed by Machiavelli, the drama of the situation is a trifle diminished. However, Strathlene offers fine views from holes which caress a heathland hillside; and at the third there is the luxury of a tiger tee perched on the cliff top reminiscent of Turnberry's famous lighthouse hole.

Two other towns a little way inland and to the west, which both benefited from the railway, were Forres and Elgin. Forres was a key junction for the Highland Railway and used to be home to more than one hundred railwaymen. The name of its football team, Forres Mechanics, stems from this connection. Locally, the town was considered Scotland's Montpellier. Developed on rising ground about the plain of Kinloss, Forres has many buildings which reflect an age of elegance and considerable prosperity.

The burghers of Forres have long enjoyed a quiet rivalry with Nairn. When in 1889 they sought to follow their neighbour's example in having a golf course of their own, they readily commandeered Nairn's foremost dignitary in Robert Finlay as their club president. They also acquired the services of Nairn's professional, Joseph Dalgleish, to lay out the course for them.

A Forres solicitor was the driving force, and it was due to his powers of persuasion that land near Kinloss bordering the Bay of Findhorn was donated by a couple of farmers. Eighteen holes were created in the Scottish fashion of straight out and straight back, sandwiched between the disused Findhorn railway and the water. Twice a day this marshy area, known as the carse, was blessed by a subterranean moisture on the ebb and flow of the tide. As a result the fairways were lush and the greens a delight.

The downside was its remote location. Kinloss station, on the Aberdeen to Inverness line, was a mile away and until the club got together a petition trains did not always stop there. Though the revenue for the return fare from Forres would have been fairly niggardly, trains then began to call at certain times of day especially for them.

Very much a plus point was the support from the Hydro health spa at Cluny Hill, close to Forres. This specialised in coldwater cures and Turkish baths. For a bulk subscription of three guineas a year their guests were also entitled to play on the course. Only when the club sought to raise this to five guineas did the hotel management dig their toes in. As a result patrons had to pay the normal green fees, modest enough in all conscience, at a shilling a day or half a crown for the week.

Ingenious publicity by the solicitor began to focus on a wider audience capable of bringing money to the town. Playing down the problems of Kinloss station, it commented on how easily Forres was reached by train – only 14 hours from London and five from Edinburgh and Glasgow. It also pointed out the area's low rainfall and how the previous year there had been 40 fewer wet days than at Nairn, a town never bashful from promulgating its climate. This supported, it was said, an old boast going back to 1640. True or not, the RAF contends that Kinloss and Lossiemouth possess Britain's best weather for year-round flying.

All the while the carse was suffering from rabbits and the spring tides. Ever so gradually its sea banks were being quietly eroded. To compound these difficulties, when one of the friendly farmers died, the agent for the estate imposed an annual charge of £5. The fee does not sound extortionate but it was more than the little club could bear. Dispirited, they terminated the employment of their greenkeeper, allowed the holes on the shoreline to fall into desuetude, and tried to make do with just nine.

Though the surviving landowner was supportive and offered further land for a new nine, the reality was that the difficulties inherent in the carse outweighed any residual will to succeed. By 1903 doom was threatening the carefree days of golfers who could gaze on the Culbin Sands, the Findhorn, the Firth, and the Sutors of Cromarty. Eventually, the friendly farmer saw no future. Reminding the club of his past generosity he requested a rental of £20. That sealed it. The club lost its course and the assets went under the hammer.

In the meantime the Hydro had engaged James Braid to design a private nine-hole course at Muiryshade right below the hotel. So cap in hand the Forres club sought agreement to play. The terms were stringent. A list of members was to be submitted with prior payment for each at 18s 6d. Next September the Hydro's course opened and presiding once again was Robert Finlay, now knighted and the Attorney General. To mark the occasion an exhibition match with a foursomes contest morning and afternoon was organised and teaming up were Harry Vardon, James Braid, the Nairn professional who had actually laid the course out, and Jack White, that year's Open Champion.

Over the next few years the Hydro was pleased with the way things were progressing and in 1911 they purchased the site with the object of remodelling the course to provide 18 holes. Willie Park was selected as architect. Following the financial collapse of Huntercombe, which he owned, he had turned to golf-course design full-time. Within the year the full 18 were ready and very popular they proved.

After the Great War, with golf at Forres continuing to pay its way, James Braid returned in 1923 to improve it further. Park, meantime, was planning or revising more than 60 courses in the USA and Canada.

In the wake of the Second World War, the fortunes of the Hydro plummeted. Hearing of the owners' disinterest, Sir Robert McVitie Grant, son of Sir Alexander of the McVitie & Price biscuit firm, bought the course and gifted it to the town, so continuing a family tradition of very great generosity. Now Forres members could play on a Sunday whereas previously this pleasure had been restricted to hotel guests.

In 1996 the wheel came full circle when, for the first time, members won the right to manage the course. Within weeks the change was noted, as trained greenkeepers took over from Council workers who were now free to tend the lawns and flowerbeds of Grant Park, another gift from this extraordinary family. Today the happy blend of undulating parkland, and heath holes winding their way through woodland, offers glimpses of Surrey or Berkshire at their best. If a few of the greens lack the finesse of the top links, one need only recall its history as an attraction for those seeking hydrotherapy. Happily, it has so far surpassed these goals and it would be a fair claim that Forres must rate as one of the finest private hotel courses built at the turn of the century.

Like Forres, Elgin, too, was a railway junction. Its prime business was similar – forwarding cattle to London's Smithfield market. Along with Keith a little further east, adjoining all three stations were cattle pens from where the local livestock auction marts were conducted. Elgin's former prosperity can be gauged by its once stately station. Converted now to offices and but for a roundabout in between, they would dwarf its modest formula-built successor.

The golf course lies on the southern fringe in open country. Here are extensive views of moorland, hills, heather and forest. Here, too, among trees that could grace any palace grounds are grand par-4 holes requiring long, straight hitting. This is some of the most testing golf in the north and a nightmare for the hooker.

In the first three holes disaster awaits. It is transparent that one's head must rule one's heart. In the middle three more holes excel: 8, 9 and 10. Again a hook will be ruinous. Finally, at the last two holes the drive must be placed with the utmost care. Perform to your handicap at Elgin and you will deserve a dram from one of the distilleries a mile or two away from the revamped clubhouse.

Part III

One early railway, which preceded the line linking Aberdeen to Inverness by six years, was the six-mile stretch between Elgin and Lossiemouth. However, had Joseph Mitchell's plan succeeded, this would have come to fruition ten years earlier still. Building on his proposals, the Morayshire Railway Company engaged James Samuel of Glasgow to implement them.

It opened on 10 August 1852 to a fandango of bands and processions in which the Provost led the way. Samuel had undertaken the civil engineering, engaged the contractor, designed the two locomotives, arranged for their building and hired the crew.

The company owned the port at Lossiemouth. In addition to passenger traffic, they saw a bright future for freight: timber out and fish back. In no time investors were rewarded for the first year's profits permitted a dividend of five per cent. But that was the only dividend they ever saw. Though the secondary intention of developing south towards Craigellachie was achieved six years later, just before Christmas, that was never to prove a commercial success.

The public's support was good but the willingness of some to pay was highly suspect. To counter this little platforms were erected outside the two termini. On-board ticket inspection was not practical since the carriages were independent and had no through corridors. So passengers were required to disembark at these makeshift stations just to show their tickets, whereupon they would clamber back in to attain their destination. With five trains a day each way and business building up, it was not long before a forty-seater third-class carriage was required. Soon that, too, was overcrowded and the company carpenter was commissioned to build a fifty-seater at not more than £135.

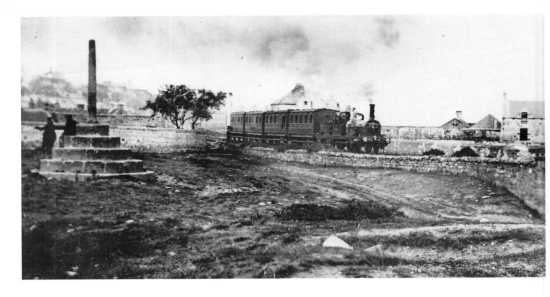

The Lossiemouth 'coffee pot' passing the old Market Cross, *c.*1882. The locomotive is
No. 4, one of the engines built in 1854 for the for the opening of the GNSR
(courtesy of the GNSR Association Collection)

The two locomotives had traditional names in *Elgin* and *Lossiemouth*
though, more popularly, they were known as the 'coffee pots'. Their
construction was unique. They carried water in a tank under the frame and as
the train moved so the water appeared to bubble. Sadly they proved light and
unreliable, and in 1857 both were damaged and the superintendent of the line
was killed. Samuel, upon whom the company now depended, was in Central
America at the time surveying a canal, and pending repairs services were
suspended.

As with Hopeman, Lossiemouth was created a model town. Sitting astride a
headland that separates two spectacular beaches, it is arguable that the winds
whistle through here even more voraciously. The GNOSR was to take over the
Morayshire Railway and when sea bathing became popular, largely on account
of Dr Grigor of Nairn, they ran a train daily for bathers convinced of the good
they would derive from an early-morning dip. The journey from Elgin took 20
minutes. Arriving at 07.00, folk had ample time to cross over to East Beach for
a run and a swim, before joining the local commuters at 08.30 on the return to
Elgin. No horse-drawn wagonette could compete since that took 45 minutes for
the single journey. Parcel business was buoyant too – so good that the local
carriers bribed Lossiemouth's station master to divert traffic to them.

It seems surprising that Lossiemouth had to wait 37 years for a proper golf course after the coming of the railways and that Strathlene and Cullen would precede it but, earlier, golf was played among the dunes though only over seven holes, and in time the little club folded due to lack of support.

In 1889 its name, the Moray Club, was resuscitated. Sixteen holes were laid out near West Beach, quickly followed by two more. This links was an immediate success and the owner of the Station Hotel in Elgin stepped in to build the Stotfield Hotel opposite the clubhouse. It was a neat double. Ever popular, the Stotfield's 16 bedrooms were added to successively so that, when he retired and his son-in-law took over, the number was approaching 70.

Next door a rival establishment sprung up in the Marine. Grandiose villas on either side were soon to become holiday homes for the rich. Some overlooked the firth while the larger ones towered above both firth and links, in some ways monstrous but never less than magnificent. It all made for an atmosphere of friendship and decorum to which people returned year after year, many of them being Scots who were making good in London.

Understandably, the club was keen to adopt the best of current practice. Players were required to wear scarlet coats embellished with dark-green collars and brass buttons bearing the club's insignia.

Naturally enough the GNOSR sought to capitalise on this upper-crust resort. Mindful that the rainfall could be as low as 19 inches and that the air was exhilarating, they gleefully promoted Lossie – as it affectionately became known – and the coastal area, as the Moray Firth Riviera. As early as 1901 they canvassed golfing holidays and sought to encourage rail travel with the issue of cheap return tickets to a variety of other courses.

Customer loyalty reached such proportions that, when the LNER succeeded the GNOSR in 1922 grouping, they readily capitalised on this by providing a special sleeping car direct to Lossiemouth from King's Cross. In so doing they established the record for the longest through service in Britain at 610 miles. The train arrived at 10.20 and the return journey was equally well timed to depart at 16.05. Consequently, a round of golf could be pursued without any problem. These were halcyon days, far removed from the club's original attitude towards members coming from Elgin. Were they to arrive late by train for a competition, it was a case of – 'Too bad: Disqualification'.

An early admirer of the course was Old Tom Morris. He had approved the design which a contractor in Forres had both suggested and implemented, and when in 1890 he came to see it for himself he was most supportive. He considered it should turn out to be the best course in the north. He envied the springy turf and the aspect of certain holes that abutted the West Beach dunes and he admired in particular how the first and last holes encroached on the town in the manner of St Andrews.

'Up to Scotland from King's Cross'
(courtesy of the National Railway Museum/Science & Society Picture Library)

The eighteenth at over 400 yards has claims to be as fine a finishing hole as any, lying as it does in a natural amphitheatre flanked on the right by steep rock gardens. The fairway is all humps and hollows. To the left are large sand traps that are shared with the first hole. However stunning the drive may be, the shot to the green requires extraordinary judgement. It is difficult to gauge the depth – actually 50 yards – for its putting surface on top of a treacherous bank is dwarfed by the clubhouse. Cavernous bunkers await a hook while an unassuming thicket of gorse takes care of any slice. This is a hole as memorable as it is tough.

In due course Lossiemouth attracted all the top golfers of the day. Harry Vardon was one, and his counsel was eagerly sought and acted upon. The professionals were bound to enjoy the bountiful hospitality of the club which included being given temporary membership. That practice started in 1910 when Lossie hosted the Scottish Professional Championship. Only 37 competed, a disappointing turnout since 62 players had taken part in the central belt the previous year and the Professional Golfers Union had arranged for discounted railway fares and cut prices at the neighbouring Stotfield Hotel.

However, the tournament found its way into the history books. In glorious weather Tom Fernie of Troon played the most astounding golf, scoring 65, a record intact until 1998. To hold a record for so long must be a record in itself, albeit that the course has since undergone various modifications. Fernie was the model of consistency with one 2 and one 5. The rest were all 3s and 4s.

The next professional tournament came early after the Great War in 1920. It was sponsored by the biscuit manufacturers McVitie & Price. Again the golf was wonderfully good and reflected Lossie's ability to bring out a player's best. Tying on 292 were James Braid and Abe Mitchell, known all his golfing life as the best player never to have won the Open. Incidentally he was the inspiration behind the design of the Ryder Cup itself, for it is a model of Mitchell that adorns the lid.

Two years later this tournament returned, very much the prestige event. First prize at £130 dwarfed that for the Open at £75. Joe Kirkwood was to win on 290. He was Walter Hagen's fellow music-hall turn and was later to gain celebrity as a trick shot artist. His trick here had been to spread-eagle the field with a first nine of 31. No one got near, and his winning margin was an indecent 13 shots.

The following year in 1923 the handsome clubhouse of 1900 was substantially enlarged to present the imposing edifice that has happily survived. The money for this came from Alexander Grant, the owner of McVitie & Price. Grant was a great benefactor. In 1920 he had offered an interest-free loan of £3,000 to build a second course, but this had been declined on the grounds of lack of need. So he offered £250 gratis to alter the first hole in line with Ted Ray's recommendations. Quite apart from the fact that the two hit it off together famously, with Ray a frequent visitor of Grant at the Marine Hotel where he maintained a suite the summer long, there was every reason why his views should count. Ray was the current U.S. Open Champion and in 1912 he had won the Open at Muirfield.

Grant was one of the two local boys to make good. Born in the 1860s he had grown up in a village near Lossiemouth. His father was a guard on the Highland Railway but Alex chose to become an apprentice baker. The other youngster to succeed was Ramsay MacDonald. His uncle had also been a guard on the Highland but his own circumstances were even more modest. His mother was in service on a farm at Alves where she became pregnant by the head ploughman. With her mother refusing to sanction marriage, the young Ramsay was brought up by the two of them – mother and grandmother. They lived in a simple two-roomed thatched cottage in Lossiemouth's Gregory Place, backing on to the railway.

At twelve he had accompanied the driver in his cab, been to sea, and worked the fields lifting tatties. Fortunately, his headmaster recognised how bright he was, enlisted him as a pupil teacher and remitted his school fees. On his death

MacDonald was bequeathed his gold watch and he wore it gratefully in pride. As the most charismatic young lad of his group, good at games and if necessary handy with his fists, his peers looked up to him. Grant was among them. They enjoyed each other's company on and off the golf course, and though Grant was never to share MacDonald's politics, the two remained lifelong friends.

While young Grant progressed from country town small bakery to be proprietor of a firm with a household name and to acquire substantial wealth, MacDonald's path to the highest office in the land had been a steady climb up the political ladder, firstly as a clerk, then as private secretary to a MP and journalist. Aided by a good marriage, active work with the Fabian society and a belief in Scottish home rule, he became leader of the Independent Labour Party. A spellbinding orator, he was all for nationalisation of land, mining royalties, and the railways!

Along the way to becoming Prime Minister of the coalition government in the 1930s, MacDonald succeeded in ruffling the feathers of certain members of the establishment at the Moray Golf Club. He suffered this with equanimity, and never wavered in his love for Lossiemouth, for he built his mother a house there and enjoyed the fresh air and relaxation of Lossie's links. When life got stressful in London, it was to Lossie that he would escape by sleeper. However, he was never accepted as a local; instead, as a Labour politican, he was regarded more as a distant MP on vacation from Leicester.

When he chose to resign the leadership because his views on war isolated him from his political colleagues, this atmosphere of diffidence changed. Passions within the golf club were ignited and in August 1915 a 'Requisition' was tabled. Ignoring the fact that he had been a radical for the best part of 30 years and a club member a good deal longer, it claimed that if MacDonald were to continue as a member of the golf club their interest would be endangered.

MacDonald challenged the motion's legitimacy. He pointed out that the Council's duties were quite divorced from any political tastes. With tongue in cheek he described their tasks as something more mundane: reprimanding members for taking dogs on to the course; preserving sobriety in the clubhouse; ensuring gentlemen insult neither ladies nor radicals; and determining penalties for rabbit scrapes, ditches, and people who play too well – that is, adjusting handicaps!

Next March the effort to dislodge him failed. That August the captain, John Foster, then Sheriff Clerk in Morayshire, tried once more. He assembled a 'Representation' complete with 30 signatures. Though his vice-captain opposed, this naïve man had not sought a seconder. So a special meeting was convened. Packed with the captain's friends it supported by 73 to 24 a motion to remove MacDonald from the role. Those attending were a trifling percentage of the membership totalling 564, and no woman was permitted to vote.

For five weeks MacDonald held his counsel. Then he wrote to the secretary, copying his letter to the press. The tone was bitter. He regretted the Moray Golf Club had become a political association with a golf course attached, that it had torn up its rules in the pursuit of spite and prejudice, and was now held up to public ridicule through the conduct of certain members, some of who were casual strangers. This was annoying for those with a claim to a peaceful holiday at Lossiemouth. The vexation was clear and the letter lacked his customary eloquence.

Never again was he to play at Lossie. The club at Spey Bay came to his aid. Appalled at the way he was treated, they conferred on him honorary membership and from then on it was here that his golf would give him lasting pleasure and here he could feel at home, though he was not infrequently also seen at Nairn as guest of his friend Grant.

In the event the ill feelings at Lossiemouth did no one any good. In no time there was a move within the club to rescind MacDonald's expulsion. The Council expressed the uneasy feeling this might not actually go far enough, since the former Prime Minister could very well snub them and decline to rejoin. So at a special meeting in Elgin's Burgh Court House a far stronger motion was tabled in favour of his reinstatement, notice of which Foster was required to send out! This was duly passed by 55 to 45 but failed to take effect because it lacked a two-thirds majority. The club was now divided and word slipped out to the press how a wealthy member who had lent it £3,000 free of interest was demanding his money back. No name was mentioned, but it would not stretch credulity to suggest it may have been Alexander Grant.

The *Manchester Guardian* decided on a scathing editorial, describing Lossiemouth's nineteenth hole as its most difficult. It deplored the expulsion of Ramsay MacDonald on account of his political views. On the other hand it entertained absolutely no doubt that every golfer in the land would have supported the club's decision had he been guilty of quite different indiscretions. Three were listed: concealing his true handicap, grounding his club in a bunker, and failing to talk interminably on his misfortune at not obtaining a four on the tenth!

The author of *Pygmalion* and who became the grand old man of letters, George Bernard Shaw, was holidaying in the Highlands at that time and the local reporter asked him for his comment. Shaw was guarded. He brooked no discussion but admitted he was bound for Lossiemouth to see what sort of place it could be that had produced the best Prime Minister of his time together with the most stupendous collection of golf snobs in history. Mischievously he suggested a memorial to both!

Embarrassment was to hover over the club like a vulture. In time it diminished but it did not disappear. When MacDonald became premier for the second time in 1929, one further effort was made to repair matters. Within days yet another special meeting in Elgin was convened. It was unequivocal. Ramsay MacDonald had been deprived of membership and was to be reinstated. Friends of the Prime Minister quickly proposed there should be no ballot, and on a show of hands not one failed to be in favour of rescinding the resolution. Elgin's paper The Courant waxed eloquent. It congratulated the club and anticipated the healing process would begin.

However the misgivings voiced by the captain five years earlier that MacDonald might decline to return proved justified. The Prime Minister saw only too clearly the club was trying to extricate itself from the fix it was in, and he made no effort to conceal he wished this had been dealt with properly many years earlier. It was now thirteen years since he had been voted out. He was happy with Spey Bay as were his friends and there he would remain!

In between times there had been a hue and cry at MacDonald's acceptance of a gift from his old friend Grant. Nosing around Somerset House a few months after MacDonald took power in 1924, a journalist discovered Grant had given him no less than £30,000 in preference shares in McVitie and Price. When shortly afterwards Grant was made a baronet, it seemed for all the world that here was MacDonald following Lloyd George in trafficking honours and, in the process, elevating a political opponent. When, too, it was discerned Grant had provided him with a magnificent Daimler so that he no longer had need to use the underground or hire a car, the press had a field day. They dubbed him a capitalist, a crook, and an enemy of society.

The explanation from both seemed genuine enough but the public was unconvinced. To Grant the car was nothing more than a necessity for one holding such high office and the interest on the £30,000 would enable him to run it. On MacDonald's death the shares were to revert to him or his heirs. As for MacDonald, he had agonised over the gift, and it had taken him a long time to be persuaded. Letters were on file to prove it.

What the press omitted to mention, if they knew it at the time, was Sir Alexander's gift of £100,000 to founding the Scottish National Library (topped up later by an equivalent amount). A baronetcy would have come his way no matter who was in power. As it was, within the year Grant felt compelled to withdraw the preference shares and the income they entailed, for he had little wish the Prime Minister should be considered beholden.

A moment's reflection shows how Foster and his ilk must have congratulated themselves on banishing MacDonald from membership. In private, tongues prattled when 'the biscuit episode', as it was known, became public.

What a different world Lossiemouth presents now. No longer do hotel guests from the Stotfield, or the Marine – for many years converted into an old people's home – take the air after dinner in black tie and long dresses, and neatly cross the road into the clubhouse for a night-cap. By day the smell of kerosene is dominant; backing on to three holes in the outward half is an active RAF airport; greenkeepers wear ear-muffs; and golfers give up momentarily and block their ears as planes, in twos and threes, take off low over the eighth green.

Fortunately there is sufficient of the old magic remaining. The course is a popular venue for the Scottish Amateur, the Home Internationals, and also the Scottish professionals. Each year the club's Golf Week in July is booked up early in January.

The springy turf will be just as Old Tom Morris knew it. The greens invariably are a delight. Gorse and burns feature and, entirely as one would expect, hidden subtleties abound. The first five holes make for a marvellous start. They are not overlong but each stroke requires careful forethought. The third is a masterpiece. The hole bends gently to the right and the green is perched high on a bank below which is Joyce Wethered's bunker to catch a shot falling short on the right. Equally the last five stay etched in the memory in offering a scenic and thrilling finish.

The Moray clubhouse overlooking the eighteenth green *(author's photograph)*

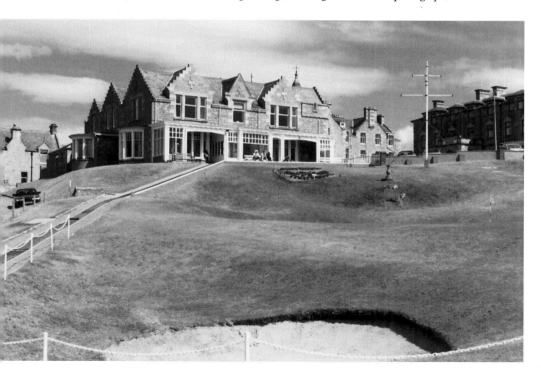

Back in the clubhouse the unspoilt view lingers. Beyond the links lie distant hills which harbour cloud. At the firthside the bay and the Covesea lighthouse beckon. Meanwhile, pool is played as others concentrate on card games, malt whisky bought by the barrel and bottled on the premises is happily consumed, and the words from that little book *Golf at its Best on the LMS* still ring true. To all appearances the modern-day Moray Club is the least pretentious place one could possibly come across.

A few miles further east, at the extremity of the good-weather belt that characterises the Moray Firth, one finds the club that offered sanctuary to MacDonald in Spey Bay. Once it was the terminus of a little branch line. Nearly as remote now as it was when first connected to rail, the golf course at Spey Bay could scarcely have got off to a more encouraging start.

The opening day was scintillating. Early September often sees the best of weather in the north of Scotland and the year 1907 was no exception. The school in Fochabers was granted a holiday and a touring circus pitched tent by the new hotel. Three thousand people turned up to witness an exhibition match between the Open Champion, Frenchman Arnaud Massy, and the ever eager Yorkshireman Sandy Herd. Of these, 600 had arrived by train from Inverness and Aberdeen.

Before a ball was struck there were ceremonies to be performed as the crowd watched intently. Firstly the Chairman thanked the Duke of Richmond & Gordon for his generosity in granting a fixed annual rental of 2s 6d for 25 years. Tactfully, and very much to the point, he hoped the Duke would profit from the feu duty of the various villas that were expected to go up near the course. Next was a presentation of a silver club and new White Flyer golf ball to Lord Walter Gordon Lennox so that he could make the inaugural drive – extremely competently as it happened. Later, out of the way of crowds engrossed with Massy's slaughter of Herd by 11 shots, 74 to 85, Lennox enjoyed a round with the Nairn's professional, Joseph Dalgleish.

Regardless that the local community of Tugnet supported barely a dozen buildings, Spey Bay was a natural place for golf. The site of the course had been known as the links, just as at Lossiemouth, for the derivation of the word signifies undulating ground on flattish coastline where turf and whins are interspersed. Virtually by definition a links will have the prospect of offering good golf. Exactly so at Spey Bay. The turf is luxurious and the huge pebble ridge that acts as a bulwark against the sea borders several tees. Pinewoods on its southern fringe furnish protection, and the humps and hollows excel those of the Royal Cinque Ports club at Deal, and even of Royal Aberdeen.

Spey Bay could very well have developed some ten years earlier, since the Great North of Scotland Railway took a careful look before opting to invest in their hotel and golfing complex at Cruden Bay. Possibly it was just too distant from Aberdeen and too much of a leap into the unknown. So it was left fallow until a committee of four with a representative from each of the nearest small towns were won over by the Spey setting. They enthused the Duke and raised the substantial capital of £2,000. (One of these settlements was Garmouth, where a charmer of a course was founded on the banks of the river Spey a few hundred yards to the west in 1931. Sadly the Spey is no friend to it now and has demolished its finest hole and necessitated adjustment to the overall design. New holes at a safer distance are but a modest substitute.)

To match their aspirations Ben Sayers of North Berwick was engaged as architect. He never quite won the Open but he was in the front rank of his generation. He paid a lightning visit. In two hours he and his flagman listened to the committee then jettisoned most of their advice. Together the two planted red-and-white flags in the whins to mark the greens and tees, where it was said, 'his deviations were awe-inspiring to the uninitiated'! His commands were followed implicitly to include the flagman taking up the post of Head Greenkeeper to see the project through.

Success was not long in coming. Sayers had a remarkable eye. With an intuitive flair he fashioned dog-leg holes of grandeur; and he chose sites for greens which not infrequently demand a ball control no less than exquisite. The short eighth and par-4 eleventh holes are superb examples. At the seventeenth the pin sits on a raised plateau. There is no bunker – even one would be superfluous. Those natural contours, humps and hollows, dunes, bent and heather, amply suffice.

Though the reputation so quickly gained was primarily due to Ben Sayers, it was well complemented. The Richmond & Gordon hotel was custom built. Resplendent with balcony, gables and a four-sided corner tower, it justified any length of journey as trains brought in holidaymakers by the score. Soon fashion took charge as wealthier patrons were to arrive in expensive hand-built cars; guests dressed formally for dinner, chauffeurs polished limousines and all was thoroughly pleasant in the manner of Brora, Dornoch and Nairn. Even rebel caddie boys did not create waves for long. With a strike threatening, their fee was upped from sixpence to sevenpence and contentment speedily reinstated.

Sadly such good times were brief. Dark clouds hung over Europe. When war broke out the hotel changed hands. Afterwards it was not quite the same, even though Ramsay MacDonald's presence and his refusal to return to Lossiemouth stood the club in good stead.

During the Second World War, troops were billeted in the hotel, land mines laid along the shore, and the formula for gracious living lapsed. With hostilities at an end, the affluent tended to look to France for their holidays and an out of the way place like Spey Bay found it difficult to escape austerity. The heady atmosphere of those early days was never to return. After Beeching axed the line

Once a magnet for the wealthy – the Richmond & Gordon Hotel, Spey Bay, during its days of splendour. The conservatory was often resplendent with geraniums *(courtesy of Jim Hutcheson)*

in 1963 and the hotel was gutted by fire two years later, restoration followed. A more modest establishment was created by infilling between what used to be the hotel's garages. It is this that serves as a home from home for visiting parties.

Yet nothing has altered the simple majesty of the setting, remote like Brancaster, with air every bit as invigorating. Maybe the greens of sea-washed turf, which were once a byword, are now too slow. But choose your day: enjoy the broad fairways and adapt to the tricky stances. Relish the richness of the heather, the wild southern hills, the songbirds and the call of the sea. Then you will readily understand that initial optimism. Though don't tell everyone. Keep Spey Bay a secret, at least until the new owners feel confident enough to blazon it abroad.

Silloth – Once a Rabbit Warren

One might well enquire how it was that in 1892 a Scottish railway company should choose to develop a first class golf course in an out-of-the-way county like Cumberland where the game was scarcely known, and then to select a rabbit warren for the purpose.

It is a convoluted story that centres on the early scramble by railway companies to gain a foothold in Carlisle. The background to all this lies in the era of the coach and horse.

Carlisle then was an important staging post not just between London and Scotland, but also for the north of England and the Lake District. In the onslaught of the railways to usurp both horse and canal, no less than seven companies were to converge on Carlisle. Of these four were English and three were Scottish. No newcomer was welcome and competition was intense. In due course the seven handled two-thirds of the Anglo-Scottish trade.

Throughout Britain the railways were winning the battle for traffic and Carlisle was no exception although, as elsewhere in the north of England, there was some reluctance to abandon the canal. The waterway to Port Carlisle was favoured by local traders since it provided some measure of independence from the combined might of the railways. It had opened in 1823 and at 11 miles long was the first stage in a grand concept to link the west coast at Maryport with Newcastle upon Tyne. That would have provided a waterway from the Irish Sea to the German Ocean. As it was, when the estimates to extend this east to Newcastle were to hand, the quotation for canal was £888 while that for rail was £252. Naturally the latter was chosen and all thoughts of the grand canal laid to rest.

In 1836 the new east-west line from Carlisle to Newcastle was opened. It stirred the imagination and a crowd of 40,000 witnessed the scene. That same year Carlisle was linked by rail to the west coast at Maryport. Few now could be in any doubt that the heyday of the canal was over.

Not that the city fathers were prepared to forego their independence. When their canal to Port Carlisle began to silt up they hit upon a novel idea. They would convert the canal bed as far as Drumburgh to a railway and this would serve as a springboard for an entirely new line to Silloth. A dock was envisaged on the deep water on the fringe of the Solway Firth which would free them from the clutches of George Stephenson's line to Maryport. To further this, in 1852 the city corporation backed the newly formed £145,000 Carlisle & Silloth Bay Dock & Railway Company.

The next year the canal was closed and drained. In a complex operation 16 bridges were raised and six locks removed. The result was a curious railway hidden in a cutting save for short, steep gradients where the locks had been.

Parliament's authority was now required for the 13 miles of new line to Silloth. Understandably the Maryport & Carlisle Railway opposed it: nobody lived in the area so there was no need for it; they could perfectly well carry all the traffic on offer; and the new line would finish in a rabbit warren! The bill was duly thrown out but following fresh lobbying was passed the next year.

The Dandy Car with soulful horse, Port Carlisle, 1900
(courtesy of Locomotive & General Railways Photographs)

In August 1856 the new line opened. For four shillings happy citizens of Carlisle had a day out. They boarded a special train and on arrival were treated to dinner at 3 p.m. in a marquee adjoining Silloth's Solway Hotel. A 'choice musical' band played rousing patriotic tunes until, replete and jolly, the party set about their return four hours later.

Performance over the line never quite matched expectations for the opposition's objections had not been without foundation. Passenger traffic on the little spur between Drumburgh and the original dock at Port Carlisle was to prove so slight that the locomotive was withdrawn and replaced by a sturdy horse, costing £35, which pulled the Dandy Car. This imaginative passenger vehicle resembled a stagecoach and had been purchased from the North British Railway after one winter's unproductive work on the line between Drem and North Berwick. It did rather better in its new home, for in the first quarter of 1898 the horse saved the company 1,887 locomotive miles!

With Port Carlisle now relegated to the horse-age, the directors focused their attention firmly on Silloth. They imagined this could be developed into a seaside resort along the lines of West Hartlepool. Heedless of the limits to the powers granted them by Parliament, they purchased 46 acres. Then they set about creating a model town with streets and terraced houses neatly conforming to a gridiron pattern.

The Caledonian Railway viewed all this with detachment. Nevertheless, as lessees of the line between Newcastle and Carlisle, they considered it in their interests to make an offer for the two companies working into Port Carlisle and Silloth. Their timing was a fraction premature. The confidence of the Carlisle men was at an all-time high, and they were rejected.

Soon the horns of a dilemma were apparent. A railway needs freight and the company had looked to the increase in passenger travel to Silloth to provide this in the future. However, before this Silloth had to be developed. Funds for this were expected to come from freight, but that was failing to materialise since the established railway companies had closed ranks. There was a cash crisis.

Salvation was to appear in 1859 through a Scottish company, the North British Railway. Their masterplan was unusual if inventive. It was to pioneer the route between Edinburgh and Liverpool as a marriage of rail and maritime, even though at the time their line only ran as far as Hawick. Once they had Parliament's authority for the Waverley route to Carlisle, which they named after the novels of Sir Walter Scott, they then could plan to continue south. Linking into the Port Carlisle & Silloth Railway they offered to generate the much-needed freight. Promises were one thing but speed of action was another. Anxious to see Silloth's railway keep in business, they gave the Silloth company's cash flow a radical boost through the avant-garde deal of buying from them their locomotives and rolling stock then leasing these back.

SILLOTH ON SOLWAY

IT'S QUICKER BY RAIL

The health resort of Silloth was vigorously promoted as evinced by this poster advertising a colourful free booklet *(courtesy of the National Railway Museum/Science & Society Picture Library)*

Cushioned by this new-found fortune, in the next couple of years the Carlisle men spent £30,000 on acquiring and developing a further 160 acres. In the process a hotel, more terraced housing, public baths and a gas works were provided. They also spent £6,000 clearing away sandhills so that a better view could be enjoyed across the Solway Firth. Determined to create the 'Torquay of the North', as the Bishop of Carlisle liked to describe it, the railway company did not hold back. They donated land for a temperance hotel, created pleasure gardens and made bathing machines freely available to boarding house proprietors. Paved roads with the charming names of Eden Street and Lawn Terrace, and a bijou green-and-white pavilion which, now the sandhills had been removed, enjoyed views across the firth, all bespoke gentrification, while a lifeboat station was to offer the feeling of security.

Carried away by their grand ambitions, matters soon came to a head. In 1862, after only six years, both Carlisle companies succumbed to the North British Railway who bought them on a 999-year lease. Their patience as suitors had paid off. The new Scottish owners not only had unfettered access to Carlisle, which for long had been blocked by the Caledonian and the London North Western Railway, they were now in a position to realise their rail/sea dream.

Promptly they purchased steamers to run from Silloth to Liverpool, Dublin and Belfast. Later they named one the *Waverley* to signify their cherished Edinburgh route through the Lowlands. One hundred and thirty years on its namesake (built in the 1940s) delights holidaymakers in the Bristol Channel and, from time to time, in the waters off the west of Scotland.

With the port now bent on becoming a steam-packet station, it made sense for the North British to carry on the development of the town as a select holiday resort. In an overtly public-spirited gesture they gave land for a church, and they imported its granite stone from Ireland free in their steamers as ballast. The cricket club was granted a site too, although once it was appreciated that waiting passengers were at risk from a ball hit for six they were asked to play bowls instead!

The chairman of the North British was an Englishman and he decided to write a colourful guidebook. This revelled in unsubstantiated claims for the climate, and extolled the ozone level as superior to that of the nearby and competing Maryport. All this was borne out by the huge sanatorium built in the sandhills beyond the harbour; although out on a limb it had its own rail spur and platform.

The private platform for Silloth's sanitorium
(courtesy of Locomotive & General Railways Photographs)

With so much investment taking place Silloth was to grow. So did the antagonism between the English and the Scots. The former retaliated by switching their traffic to Maryport a few miles to the south. Lacking this patronage, the port of Silloth was deprived of its full potential. Slowly the North British lost interest: and that was accentuated once they could run freight between England and Scotland over the Settle to Carlisle line. To their shame they grew curmudgeonly, refusing even to maintain the sewers or to provide a public urinal. Silloth had become peripheral to their core business. It scarcely seemed worth bothering with.

In the further passage of time it dawned on them the town could be worth cultivating as a tourist centre. When the fashion for golf took hold in the 1890s the company decided to release some of their surplus land for a course. The site for this bordered the firth and lay beyond the dock and station. It was the rabbit warren referred to nearly 40 years earlier by the Maryport & Carlisle Railway!

Carlisle station in its heyday with a Carlisle locomotive No. 735 in pristine condition, 1898 (*courtesy of Locomotive & General Railways Photographs*)

Quite coincidentally the North British had a special and unusual relationship with golfer Willie Park Jnr. One of their lines ran through his property and in return he was able to flag down any passing train. Naturally Willie was invited to lay out the course.

Money was no object. Only the best quality turf was used and, together with his uncle Mungo and local man David Grant, the three ensured great pains were taken over the preparation of the greens.

The outcome is wonderful natural golf as unconstrained as Machrihanish and Brora. Just to tread on the yielding turf is a delight. Humps and hollows abound, with several converted into pot bunkers barely large enough for four sheep or a courting couple. Blind shots are not abhorred. Greens lurk in bowls as they do at Machrie on Islay, or sit astride pinnacles. It matters not. Variety is all and nature has been generous. Hillsides house plantations of gorse, fairways appear isolated as swathes among heather, and carries over wilderness necessitate a still head and a watchful eye. Only the patient can expect to return to the clubhouse duly rewarded.

Park must have taken the greatest pleasure in Silloth, arguably the first course of the highest class he had designed on his own. The last hole is well worthy of what has gone on before. It is a tough par 4 overseen by terraced cottages whose lace curtains shield windows behind which one can imagine furtive glances along with the smell of kippers for tea. Somehow they take on the air of a grandstand at a small country racecourse. To some extent the clubhouse on the other side of the green also shares this situation, although it is from the dock side and the former station yard that it looks its most captivating, squat but proud upon an embankment.

Despite Cumberland's considerable distance from the expanding world of golf, Park's course was not the first that Silloth had seen. In the early 1870s the local Doctor Leitch had knocked a ball around on the green in front of the parish church. This encouraged him to lay out nine holes on the foreshore. He was closely followed by Willie Fernie who designed a short course to appeal to holidaymakers. However, it was Park's course that was to catch the eye of the founding medical fraternity of Carlisle's golf club at Dalston. Urged on by Dr Leitch, the two clubs merged, the Carlisle doctors no doubt also motivated by the leasehold charge from the North British of only £1 per annum.

Leitch had the good fortune to father five daughters. All were athletic and were keen on golf, and three went on to become internationals. These were Edith, May and Cecilia, nicknamed Cecil. Edith was English Ladies Champion in 1927 but it was Cecil who stole most honours. She was the only lady who could challenge Joyce Wethered in her prime. Most emphatically she was good for the course and because of her prowess any golfer worth his salt could tell you where Silloth was!

Cecil won the Ladies Amateur Championship four times, the French five times, the English twice and the Canadian once. She was capped for her country no less than 12 times on either side of the Great War, and she held 20 course records. Apart from the five years of war she was also out of golf for the whole of 1923 as she rested the muscles she had torn in her forearm the previous year during a tour of the USA and Canada.

Known for her palm-under grip, and ducking right knee, Cecil attacked the ball with heavyweight clubs. It was always said that Joyce could not bear to watch her for fear of losing her rhythm. Yet Cecil was feminine enough to wear a bow in her hair when young, and cute enough not to succumb to fashion if it meant wearing a heavy woollen skirt that would impede her whirlwind swing. A lady at Cooden Beech was not so forward thinking; it rained and her knitted skirt sagged. Absorbing the moisture, it became so heavy she could hardly walk, let alone play. As a result she had to be allowed to change before tackling the final hole! In contrast Cecil's skirts were commonly of men's tweed, with a generous width to accommodate her individualistic knee action.

Punchy, tall and strong, her attitude was quite different to that of Joyce. Cecil liked to practise the shots she could play well since this gave her confidence a lift. Joyce on the other hand regarded that as a terrible waste of good shots, reckoning there was a distinct limit to how many there were in any one locker. Later in life Cecil became a formidable antiques dealer, while Joyce chose the rather more gentle occupation of gardening with which she could indulge her fondness for roses.

Entirely as predicted, the relative success of Silloth as a holiday centre and port was to spell doom to Port Carlisle. Following the example of Silloth's passenger services some 40 years earlier, in 1899 the locomotive-hauled freight services to Carlisle ceased and were replaced by a horse – a system which was kept in operation until 1914. As for the old Dandy Car, that had become the pavilion for the Silloth bowling club. Later this unique vehicle was restored and exhibited, firstly at Edinburgh Waverley and then at Carlisle; it is now in the National Railway Museum at York.

At the time of the Grouping, when on 1 January 1923 Britain's railways were channelled into four companies, Cumberland's lines passed to the LMS. All, that is, except one – the line between Carlisle and Silloth with the spur off to Port Carlisle. Together with the other North British lines this went to the LNER.

They strove to take advantage of their newly acquired west-coast outlet in encouraging Geordie visitors from Tyneside by means of Saturday specials. These then linked in to steamer services for the Isle of Man and Dublin. Silloth's golf, too, was avidly promoted even by the LNER's own high standards. Poster advertising was all the rage. One showed a young woman silhouetted against the

LNER's romantic poster for Silloth
*(courtesy of the National Railway
Museum/Science & Society Picture
Library)*

sea and the sky. She swings gracefully in the style of Henry Cotton among Silloth's dunes and humps and hollows as, quite shamelessly, realism gives best to romanticism.

The club was able to buy their course in 1937, but for a good 30 years Silloth was to retain a soft spot among railwaymen and the travelling public. In 1954 its branch line became the first where the DMU (diesel multiple unit) superseded steam. Alas success did not follow.

In September 1964, when Doctor Beeching wielded his axe, the reaction was rabid. Nine thousand angry, jeering people packed the little terminus. Dozens sat on the line delaying the last train by half an hour. An inspector was stoned. Detonators were placed on the track and British Rail was ruffled.

They responded by lifting the tracks afterwards so speedily that several carriages were marooned. At unnecessary expense these had later to be dismantled and carted away by low-loader on the highway.

It was a galling finale. In little over a century those fine dreams of the independent-minded Carlisle men had evaporated. The lasting reminder of their canny Scots successors proved to be not a railway, but an unprepossessing dock long since devoid of steamer services and, far, far better, the most marvellous conversion ever of a rabbit warren into a golf course – quite literally a little piece of Scotland over the border. Little wonder that it is the pearl of Cumbria!

Golf on the LNER

Golf was originally played with the feathery ball. It did not fly particularly far and it was costly for it took half a day to make each one by hand. But in 1850, when the gutta-percha ball was invented, matters altered radically. The new ball travelled further, lasted longer and was cheaper. In consequence the game became more popular and the number of golf courses began to increase. From just a few score, by 1886 that total had grown to 171, with many of the more recent ones being close to a railway.

'Cruden bay by East Coast Route'
(courtesy of the National Railway Museum/Science & Society Picture Library)

Then the game mushroomed. Golf and rail were seen to be good for each other and in ten years the number of courses jumped six-fold. In 1896 there were well over a thousand courses throughout Britain.

Over each one of the next half-dozen years growth was steady averaging six new courses every month. Then in 1903 the pace accelerated again, no doubt due to the introduction of the Haskell ball with its core of rubber thread wound tightly under tension. This afforded so much more feel and pleasure than the solid core gutty. As with the feathery which it had replaced, that too rapidly became obsolete.

Even allowing for a period of consolidation, in 1914 Nisbet's *Directory of Golf Clubs* was to list some 2,844. Despite the motorcar now finding favour with the well-to-do, against each entry Nisbet's guide still recorded the distance from the station either in quarters of a mile or in minutes. Where more than one station was involved, both its name and that of the railway company were detailed.

This was an inspiration to the LNER who chose to woo golfers through a remarkable pocket book called *A Round of Golf on the London & North Eastern Railway*. Their choice as author could not have been better. In Bernard Darwin they selected a railway enthusiast, a golf fanatic and a man of letters. His foreword neatly sums up its aspirations:

> This little book contains accounts of various golf courses on the LNER. Some of them I have known long and intimately . . . but all have pleasant and friendly memories for me. I hope that perhaps other people may be tempted to go and play on some of these and, if they do that they enjoy them as much as I did.

The first course to get a mention was Cruden Bay; several miles north of Aberdeen it necessitated the longest train journey that was detailed out of London.

Here, in 1893 a company, later absorbed into the LNER under the 1922 Grouping, had taken a bold step. The previous year the first-ever golf course built by a railway company had been opened at Silloth. Now their Scottish rivals, in the form of the Great North of Scotland Railway, were to follow suit in obtaining powers to build a hotel, a golf course and a connecting railway line running from Ellon to the fishing port of Boddam. They would have preferred that the line continued the final three miles through to Peterhead, but the Highland Railway opposed such a move. As it was, the overall objective was unimpaired, namely to develop Cruden Bay and Port Erroll as seaside resorts.

In August 1897 this new, fifteen-and-a half-mile-long line opened. By then the golf course was already laid out, designed by Old Tom Morris and supervised by Archie Simpson. A deal had been done with the proprietor of Hayfarm which involved the tenant farmer Alexander Castel giving up his

Poster advertising the *Holiday Handbook*, 1,140 pages of illustrations, maps, street plans and places to stay in Cruden Bay *(courtesy of the National Railway Museum/Science & Society Picture Library)*

grazing rights over the link pasture and the bent-hills, as well as relinquishing over 16 acres of good arable land. In return he received £40 per annum until his lease expired on Whit Monday 1911.

Eighteen months later the hotel opened in March 1899. Built in the local red granite and with 96 bedrooms, from afar it had all the appearances of a fortress on the edge of the Sahara. Soon all knew it as 'The Palace in the Sandhills'. Its attractions included tennis, croquet and bowls, and the ladies had a little nine-hole course of their own. The directors and senior officers of the company were so convinced of the venture's wisdom they were to offer a champagne lifestyle – quite literally. A supply for the hotel was sanctioned in November 1897, well in advance of the hotel's opening, to allow time for the bottles to mature further. They included 50 dozen each of Pommery 1893 'Nature', Moet et Chandon 1893 Cuvee 81, and Mumm 1893 Extra Dry. The prices were indicative of their reputations. Respectively, they were 83s, 71s 5d and 68s 4d per dozen. In February 1901 Ayala was bought at 76s 6d together with Veuve Clicquot 1893. That fetched a premium, firstly at 91s then at 93s. Meanwhile Pommery's price had risen to 110s, but the Board decided to hold back and retain the bottle price ex-cellars at 14s 6d!

A year later their champagne purchase was even more sophisticated. Ignoring the London and Liverpool wine trades they obtained 50 cases of Louis Roederer's 1898 vintage at 65s a dozen FOB French port.

The grandeur of the establishment can be gauged from the hotel's valuation for fire insurance purposes. The total came to £41,500, and of this £21,000 was for the building, £8,700 for the furniture and plate, and £1,000 for the cellar stock and cigars. Bedding and linen were seemingly modest at £350. In contrast the electric bells and telephones were highly rated at £1,800.

Along with the hotel Cruden Bay was granted a showpiece station for the well-heeled guests. Aiming to capivate passengers on their very first impression of Cruden Bay, the station was far more lavish than its neighbours along the line at Auchmacoy, Pitluig, Hatton or Longhaven. An extravagant glass canopy sought to protect the platform from the area's none too certain climate. This doubled as the terminus for a tramway which was completed three months after the hotel but just in time for the summer season. It was to convey visitors direct but also carried goods consisting of coal, stores and all the GNOSR laundry in between times. Seeking economy of scale the company utilised the hotel's splendid new facilities for cleaning all their uniforms, tablecloths and antimacassars. Three trailer vehicles were required for the goods while two single-deck tramcars sufficed for the passengers. All were built in the GNOSR company's carriage works.

Famous names were attracted to Cruden Bay for happy family holidays. Among them were Sir William Burrell the shipowner, whose fabled art collection is housed in Glasgow's Pollok Park; the Colmans of Norwich who made mustard; the Crawfords who baked biscuits; the Gilbeys who distilled gin and imported French wines; the McEwans who brewed beer; and the Wills of Bristol who made cigarettes. Little wonder then that up to a hundred schoolboys would be begging the caddymaster for employment, hoping to curry favour, or at least be a member of the winning team in contests where bisques and calls of 'woof' – generally made by light-hearted siblings – contributed to the hilarity of holiday golf.

The columnist Bernard Darwin was equally entranced. After complimentary remarks on the five-storey turreted hotel he was to write:

> The visitor sees one of the most entirely inviting golfing views in the world. There are ranges of sandhills, one beyond the other, promising all sorts of tremendous carries and hidden hills. Beyond them is the Bay of Cruden with

rocks and seagulls and fine creamy waves, and inside them is a really beautiful bit of golfing country, broken and undulating and eventful.

A few paragraphs later he is citing the turf as almost too good:

in that the ball sits up just asking to be hit and so deludes the player into a belief that he has permanently improved with his brassie.

The London Midland & Scottish Railway was also to acknowledge the attractions of Cruden Bay. Though they had no involvement in the local line, they ran services to Aberdeen 23 miles to the south and were concerned that they, too, obtained their share of long-distance golfing passengers. In 1925 they emulated the LNER in commissioning a book called *Golf at its Best on the LMS*. This tells at first hand of leading courses which the author knew. He wrote with a dry sense of humour unashamed of the poetic licence in the title, for on finally reaching Cruden Bay he allowed himself the observation, 'Surely, there is no golf here.' Blind to the beauty of the imposing station he equated it to the back of beyond, and with a nice side-swipe at the LNER compared it to a depot for milk churns!

Once at the hotel and warmed by a drink his perception changed. Remembering that he was there to drum up business for the LMS, he made it sound so thoroughly enticing. Awaking to the 'swish, swoosh, ping' of the waves, he was to see the caddymaster before breakfast and book 'a vigilant lad for the long day's golfing idyll'.

Despite the purple prose and considerable promotional efforts, the entire venture never once succeeded in financial terms. A £70 salary for Alex Weir, professional, club-maker and greenkeeper, seemed excellent value, and £25 to support the golf club in 1901 was no burden. Neither was £37 to extend the croquet lawn. However, the auguries were not good. With the experience of just one winter, it was only after careful consideration that the hotel was kept open during the following winter of 1900/01 and even then to attract business a special winter tariff at £2 10s a week had to be introduced.

Meanwhile there was friction behind the scenes and an air of disappointment. Miss Campbell, the manager of less than two years, resigned. Offering three months' notice she was let go the next day with three months' pay. Her successor fared no better. Miss Frater survived 16 months before being dismissed. The hunt was then on to find a replacement and so the £100 salary was more than doubled, though in the event a manager and housekeeper were appointed at £130 and £80, so inflating the costs still further.

In fact the hotel never paid for itself and neither did the railway built specifically to make it accessible. The season was too short, and the fish traffic

LONDON & NORTH EASTERN RAILWAY.

GENERAL MANAGER'S OFFICE (SCOTLAND),
EDINBURGH, 12*th October* 1932.

CIRCULAR $\frac{G.M.}{243}$

Suspension of Passenger Train Service on Cruden Bay Branch.

The Staff are hereby informed that the Passenger Train Service at the undernoted Stations will be withdrawn during the winter months, as from Monday, 31st October, 1932.

Auchmacoy	Cruden Bay
Pitlurg	Bullers o' Buchan (Halt)
Hatton	Longhaven
Boddam	

Detailed instructions relating to Parcels and Goods Traffic will be issued in due course by the Officers concerned.

J. CALDER,
General Manager, Scotland.

Circular advising of the suspension of passenger service on the Cruden Bay branch

from Boddam destined for market at Aberdeen failed to reach expectations and achieve the freight budget. Though the basic frequency of five trains each way daily varied, the forty-minute journey was as constant as the red figures. It was not long before recriminations flew, the judgement of the officers was called into question, and all concerned wished that the plans had never got off the drawing board. Even running a Sunday service at discounted tickets had been criticised as encouraging the desecration of the Sabbath through playing golf! The local newspaper defended the GNOSR for 'beguiling a lot of idle fellows out to Cruden Bay' where it was thought 'they will be just as well employed . . . as loafing abut church doors and annoying worshippers'.

No matter what, the exercise had failure written all over it. In 1932 the railway line closed to passenger traffic. The tramway ceased in 1941. Then, after being put to good use as a hospital, the hotel was shut down in 1945. At 96 bedrooms it was too big to justify refurbishment for a three-month tourist season and, in any case, tastes were changing. In preference to the chill and wind of the north-east coast, the better-off families were being drawn to the Continent. As a result, the new owners razed it to the ground; 'The Palace in the Sandhills' had bitten the dust. Hardy Aberdonians were untroubled. They continued to enjoy Cruden Bay's wonderful golf on a course that in 1997 was good enough for the British Ladies Amateur Championship.

Of that railway line conceived with such high hopes there is scant trace, an anomaly all the more marked when one considers how those prosperous families, who were the hotel's early patrons, are remembered as brand names for consumer goods pretty well the world over.

Another Scottish course to feature in the LNER pocket book was North Berwick. The name 'Norberwic' dates back to Viking times. Indeed, surnames of Viking extraction remain prevalent on Scotland's east coast. It was also known as 'The Biarritz of the North', possibly to be one up on Nairn which was called 'The Brighton of the North'.

Though remote it had long prospered from the cultivation of barley, and its status was recognised as early as 1373 when Robert II designated it a royal burgh. However, after the Reformation came dark days and a reputation for sorcery, witchcraft and plots against the King. Early in the nineteenth century large landowners dominated and the atmosphere remained feudal. Indeed,

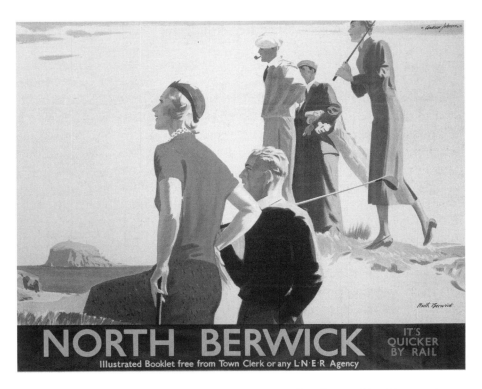

Poster promoting North Berwick as holiday resort; a free illustrated booklet was also available *(courtesy of the National Railway Museum/Science & Society Picture Library)*

when golf was first played there in 1832, North Berwick was as remote as ever – the journey by stagecoach from Edinburgh took a good three hours.

Ten years later the North British Railway Company was formed. Its objective was to build a line from Edinburgh to Dunbar then, on completion, to extend it to the border town of Berwick-upon-Tweed. Progress was rapid and within two years Edinburgh golfers were able to take the train to Drem. There a stagecoach would be waiting to take them on. Though suggestions of building a line from Drem to North Berwick initially drew short shrift, the company embarked on the venture nevertheless, in what was a defensive measure designed to prevent inroads into their territory by a would-be competitor – the East Lothian & Tyne Valley Railway.

It was an expensive gesture costing £75,000 and misgivings were soon to follow. In 1849 an independent committee was to tell shareholders of their regret this had ever come about. Still, by next June North Berwick was fully linked into the railway system and, not least, the local fishermen were delighted. Business was plentiful, for in a season they were averaging 12,000 barrels of herring on top of such delicacies as lobster and crab. Now they could tap in to the markets of London, Birmingham and Leeds.

In November 1856 golfers venturing off to North Berwick were treated to the Dandy Car. Rather like a stagecoach on four large wheels, it represented a handsome example of early lateral thinking. As with the local carrier's coach, over which it offered no real advantage, additional seats were on the outside. That was where the driver sat, for the Dandy was horse-drawn! Though chic, it was too cramped to be popular. So the North British withdrew it, whereon it languished for three years. Then in a crafty move they sold it to the Port Carlisle & Silloth Railway to work a spur line to Carlisle's port. Years later, when they eventually took them over, they were to regain their cast-off possession.

In 1859 the North British exercised considerable foresight when they entered into partnership with the owner of North Berwick's Royal Hotel. Both sides did so well the relationship lasted 64 years. When their successor company, the LNER, was to sell its interest, they realised the tidy sum of £8,500.

By now North Berwick possessed three more hotels and had acquired the status of a highly desirable watering place. Wealthy families were drawn to the area and many chose to stay for months on end. The more magnificent houses that overlooked the links and the Firth of Forth found ready tenants and, from their elevated situations, the Bass Rock and Fife's ancient fishing villages positively glistened in the brittle light. Comparison with bracing Biarritz, if not justified, was at least understandable.

Golf was seen as good for the North British. Those imbued with the bug were providing an affluent and growing market. As a result the company was happy enough to build a small halt just short of the terminus for players' convenience. Long-distance travellers were courted too. Commencing in 1913 two through carriages operated all summer long from London's King's Cross. Then in 1924 a first-class sleeper service ran nightly with one coach detaching at Drem. This continued up to 1939. After the war the situation was slightly different; however, golfers for North Berwick, along with its august neighbours of Muirfield and Gullane, were still catered for since the Edinburgh sleeper service called at Drem. This lasted until 1980 despite all onward connections by rail or bus having long disappeared. With patronage now minuscule the call was cut out.

It was in the 1890s that North Berwick had risen to be Scotland's premier east-coast resort. Even had he not been born a few miles away at Whittinghame in East Lothian, it was natural that it should have been the regular haunt of A. J. Balfour, Britain's golfing Prime Minister, caricatured by *Punch* as Mr Golfour. His grandfather hailed from Fife and had made his fortune in India. On his return, he purchased an estate of 14,000 acres that became the family seat. Balfour's father was the MP for nearby Haddington, the Commanding Officer of the East Lothian Yeomanry Cavalry, and a director of the North British Railway. His mother, Lady Blanche Cecil, was the daughter of the second Marquess of Salisbury. If anyone had entered the world clutching a silver spoon, it was A. J.

With the pick of the country's golfing resorts from which to choose, seldom did he doubt the wisdom of returning here for the long summer recess, though once he confided to his lifelong friend Lady Elcho, daughter of Lord Wemyss at nearby Gosford:

> I am not looking forward to North Berwick (or golf) quite as normal, partly because the people I want will not be there, partly because the people I do not want, will. Among the latter class I emphatically rank . . . a Manchester MP . . . He ruins everything by an intolerable mania for telling stories . . . usually old and always dull, with which he pursues his flying friends and which he pours in an unceasing stream into any ear that comes handy . . . I know with a certain prescience he will render life intolerable.

Those in the public eye acquire many advantages, but a certain sympathy is due Balfour in having to share his holiday rendezvous with such a bore.

Darwin's little book steers well clear of personalities, other than Balfour himself, and his admiration for North Berwick lay in its subtleties. He pinpointed the need in summer for deft pitching, when the ground gets hard, the greens become fiery, and an overbold ball will bound towards the sea. He recalled:

This is painfully true of the first hole, Point Garry Out, and I always remember a newspaper account of Mr – as he then was – A. J. Balfour's beginning a medal round: 'The Premier made an unfortunate start: put his second on the rocks and took eight to the hole.'

As would be expected, he makes mention of Perfection, a hole which hugs the dunes and calls for a carefully flighted second shot over an old stone wall if the ball is to settle on the green. The Redan he describes as shy with its intricacies. Yet this is as famous as any Scottish short hole and much copied in America. He ends by noting how the course is rightly popular, and he stresses the need for rhythm and tempo:

> In the height of the season the round may have taken us a good three hours, but as to that I think North Berwick is like St Andrews; it has a remarkably soothing effect on the most impatient temperaments. You know how long it will take before you start: you know that it does not matter whether you have two wholly incompetent ladies in front of you or two Open Champions. You will go just the same pace of the green. And so you cease to fret and fume, and enjoy the good golf and the sunshine and the view of the Bass with a reasonable placidity.

Of those golfing Meccas for which Drem station was the destination, Muirfield was to symbolise the carriage trade, being home to the Honourable Company of Edinburgh Golfers. On the other hand Gullane Hill was the setting for a variety of clubs and societies drawn from a wider spectrum. Some went by flamboyant names: the Hanky Panky Golfers, the Roundel Club, the Harum Scarum Club, the Gullane Nine, and the Gullane Comrades. Little surprise then that when trains first plied the Gullane branch in 1898, popularity for golf on the Hill took a further leap forward.

Not that the game there was in any way new, for golf of a sort had been played in this heaven-sent environment since 1650. One early challenge was that between Dirleton's weavers and those of Aberlady. Surrounded by good farming land, sheep were the source of much prosperity. Indeed, with distilleries not to feature for another generation or two, Scotland's principal export until 1800 was wool.

Local farmers would also enjoy each other's company, but around 1848 their club folded. With the gutta percha ball then replacing the feathery, the club rose again like a phoenix under the name the East Lothian Golf Club. Small matter that in 1855 they had been pre-empted by the Dirleton Castle Club. Composed mainly of shopkeepers and artisans, in no way did this inhibit the farmers' fun. Gastronomy was just as important as golf! On becoming habitués of the Golf Hotel, the landlord was kindly asked to serve his whisky and sherry in decanters not quite so like each other for, as the evening wore on, it was claimed, 'some of the members found it very difficult to distinguish which was which'.

He must have responded positively since eight years later in 1896, after the Spring Meeting it was to here the members repaired in late afternoon to dine. The fare was excellent, toasts were drunk, witty speeches were delivered and a singsong ensued the entire coach drive to Drem. There, camaraderie grew so strong that when the Edinburgh train arrived, a dozen piled into a carriage for six so celebrations could continue unabated.

Almost lost in the mists of time is a tiny piece of history. For 600 years Gullane was a minor ecclesiastical centre. Its importance long ended, golf was to revive the small community with play around the old St Andrews Church on three (later seven) holes. But distraction took the form of the galloping horses being trained on the course and only after recourse to law in 1892 was the matter resolved. Gullane Hill was to be solely for golf. Horses were banished.

The catalyst for improvement was already in place for ten years earlier a club bearing the village name had been founded. With the course now 18 holes, the clubhouse was opened in 1889. Members posed gleefully for a photographer and *The Courier* was to record, 'a more manly and intellectual set of men no one need to desire to look upon'. No comparison with the elitist Honourable Company was offered!

In 1898 Gullane gained its own station and a new branch line provided direct access from Edinburgh. A second course was now deemed appropriate and Willie Park Jnr. of Musselburgh was invited to advise. Paying three visits he submitted his account for ten guineas. The committee was prudent. They demurred and Mr Park was requested to modify the sum. Willie would do nothing of the sort. His demands were not excessive. He was to be paid in full. And he was. As he should have been in the first place! Indeed, Gullane Number 2 is an unsung but entirely typical example of what masterly golf Scotland can offer in air like wine.

Now everything went swimmingly. The North British Railway took over the local line and the number of visitors increased. A third course followed Gullane Number Two ten years later. In fact there were four on the Hill if one includes (Old) Luffness. Sweetness and light reigned, quite the equal of the spectacular views that rival clubs enjoy only in part, namely the mighty tracery of the Forth Bridge, the tiny islands and ships which dot the firth, and the pleasant slopes of Fife beyond. To the south the Lammermuir Hills shield acres of barley and of corn; the beauty overall being enough to distract even Joyce Wethered.

Between the wars the club was able to purchase all the land it required. With this came a share in crops fringing the courses and a £60 fee from the rabbit trapper. By 1939 he was on the greenstaff and the steward's wife was adept at rabbit recipes. As for the once convenient railway, that had ceased at the beginning of the decade. With traffic relatively light, the journey by car from Edinburgh involved no great strain.

Perhaps the last comments on Gullane should belong to Bernard Darwin. He enjoyed the challenge of emulating the Duke of York: the marching up to the top of the hill, the march down again, and all the while taking care not to stray from one course on to another. He recalled the lovely turf that could put a spring into the most leaden foot; the baby rabbits that whisked their frightened little white tails in and out of the rough, the piping of the gulls and the sensation that one was playing in a little world of one's own – 'our's and the gulls' and the rabbits'.' He was to enthuse that there was no other golfing centre quite so good as Gullane – a view to stand the test of time.

A club that has never sought publicity and where members are happy with their own company is Panmure at Barry. Originally they enjoyed their golf over the adjoining links at Monifieth. It was there in 1845 that two noted St Andrews men, Allan Robertson and Alexander Pirie, laid out the initial nine holes for a modest fee of 30 shillings. With the local landowner Lord Panmure agreeing to be Patron the club pedigree could not be faulted.

For £2 10s a little golf house was rented. Like the golf course it was right by the railway which had opened seven years earlier. When an increase in charge was requested, the club suggested to the Dundee & Arbroath Railway company that while they were constructing a nice little station at Monifieth they might kindly furnish a room for the Panmure members. That was readily agreed. What is more – and this is probably quite unique – as numbers increased they undertook to build Panmure a totally new clubroom, right behind the station and one minute away from the first tee. So keen was the Board to encourage business to the line from Dundee and Broughty Ferry, they accepted a rental negotiated down from 7^{1}/2% to 3^{1}/2% on a capital cost not exceeding £200. They must have been satisfied with their £7 a year, because when the club asked if they might buy the building they declined the offer.

In 1857 there was a move by the members to switch from Monifieth to Carnoustie. However, the site they had in mind for a clubhouse clashed with Lord Panmure's own plan for a bathhouse; and this time the railwaymen were not so co-operative. They saw no reason to pay for a new clubhouse, and were not prepared to rent out any of their existing buildings. In the event the idea failed. The members stuck with Monifieth and in the course of time commissioned a new clubhouse conveniently sited on railway property.

In the 1890s the club was given the opportunity to purchase the links; an offer which they turned down. So in stepped the town council who snapped it up for £4,000. When a hotel was proposed immediately in front of their clubhouse so as to spoil its view, the Panmure men took umbrage and the notion of vacating Monifieth was revived.

Allan Robertson, a supreme
golfer in the 1840s and 1850s

In 1900 they moved to Barry. Here the original Patron's descendant, the Earl of Dalhousie, was happy to sell them 110 acres for £1,510. While far cheaper than Monifieth, it was not ideal. The holes run in a narrow confine, basically westward out and eastward home. One Colonel Henderson did not mince his words:

> The Course is of the most unpromising looking ground from a Greenkeeper's point of view consisting of large hummocks and deep ravines with marshy looking bottoms, and covered with the coarsest of bent grass, whins and rushes; but to the Golf Architect giving promise of many sporting holes and shots.

The railway company now renamed Barry Station calling it Barry Links. Golfers' return tickets from Dundee were available in the clubhouse and cost one penny. To meet the demand on early closing day, Wednesdays, a special stop was inserted at 11.40 on the train off Dundee and at 15.17 on the way back. Members either walked the few hundred yards or took advantage of a small dogcart. Caddies met the trains and earned an extra sixpence on top of their normal fee to hump the clubs and any hand luggage. As for the new clubhouse, it was modelled on Royal Calcutta, the prime refuge for members of India's jute trade and with whom Dundee had the closest ties.

Both enjoy a sybaritic style which has survived. Panmure offers leather armchairs, warm panelling, fine silver, linen serviettes and excellent house wine. High expectations of the catering are upheld. After lunch, as at Prestwick, one faces a choice of port or kümmel. The port is served in a 20cl bottle rather than by the glass and since three of these suffice nicely for four persons, the art of pouring is monitored most carefully. Four pairs of eyes are lowered to the same height as the glasses to ensure the allocation for each is identical. Up and down they go until all four are satisfied the measurements are exact.

As for the golf course, the railway is visible throughout. Large tees appear immaculate. Greens are subtle and occasionally wicked. One can only hope and pray that the greenkeeper charged with choosing the pin positions feels kindly towards his fellow men and enjoys a happy home life. The short holes are demanding and require the most thoughtful club selection.

The sixth and twelfth holes are especially memorable. They offer target golf of the highest order, with the Buddon Burn at its most sinuous on the latter. There it waits patiently, rather like a crocodile intent on ensnaring some morsel for elevenses or, indeed, any time of day. An added bonus is the masterly contribution of Ben Hogan. The villainous sand trap that he suggested at the

Ben Hogan at Wentworth. Seated to his left is the author, arms crossed and not yet 21
(*courtesy of* Golf World)

sixth, positioned at 4 o'clock below a heathery hillock, is known as Hogan's bunker.

Alone among the stars preparing for the Open at Carnoustie in 1953, he was permitted to practise at Panmure. Quietly, well away from prying eyes he persevered, even mowing the seventeenth green himself, with blades lowered, to achieve a pace approaching that prevailing on the championship links a mile away on the other side of the tracks. Grateful for the opportunity, he cleaned the mower afterwards before handing it back to the head greenkeeper.

As all golf students will know, Hogan went on to win, with each score improving on the round before. Not that it was his putting which saw him good, rather it was his utterly devastating long game and meticulous placing of each shot. In its own way Panmure encourages that too, aided no doubt by the improving hand of James Braid. As with the clubhouse the links will satisfy the particular. The promise of many sporting shots and holes is amply fulfilled.

In that first edition of his LNER book, Darwin wrote up 23 courses. This proved such a success he added more. His problem was to be selective. Golf courses now isolated from rail, like the two English jewels of Ganton and Woodhall Spa, were at that time a few minutes casual stroll from the local station. His book listed every course in England and Scotland that was served by a LNER station, it detailed the ongoing distances, and gave the name and address of each club's secretary. In Scotland reduced fares were available and he quoted their cost from Aberdeen, along with such helpful advice as the off-peak days in summer, and where to get hold of the coupons offering discounts for the rail journey and cups of tea. Also listed were the green fees and all 25 of the LNER's hotels.

By now the very name London North Eastern Railway was a misnomer. The company had extended west from the cool and breezy east coast to serve Lanark, Dumbarton, Bute, Argyll, and even Carlisle and Silloth following its absorption of the North British. What is incontrovertible is that no railway company operating out of London ever tried harder to promote golf in order to win more passengers to its services. Their focus on this equalled that of the golf-loving Scots.

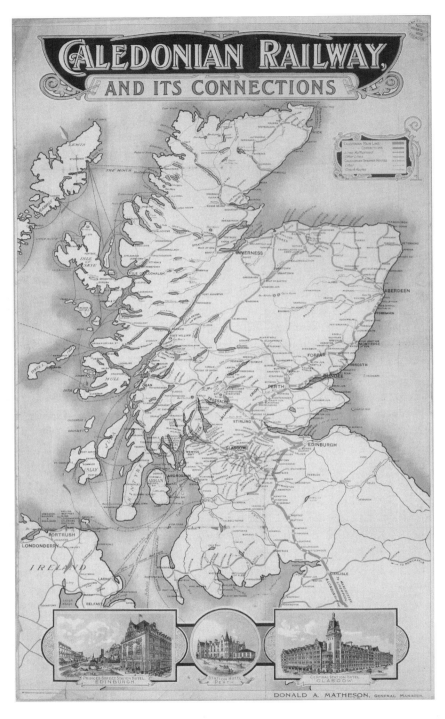

The Caledonian Railway and its connections *(courtesy of the National Railway Museum/Science & Society Picture Library)*

Gleneagles – Enchanted Ground

In the Edwardian era to stay at a railway hotel by a golf links was considered the hallmark of success, for they were the epitome of good living and good taste. Unrivalled, they were in a class of their own. The Caledonian Railway Company had long known a thing or two about the hotel business. In 1885 they had opened Glasgow's Central Hotel and they followed this with the Caledonian Hotel in Edinburgh in 1903. Yet the anomaly was that while the railway had put the Scottish Highlands within reach, railway-owned hotels there were scarce and the Caledonian was bereft.

In 1910 the company's new General Manager, Donald Matheson, was holidaying at Strathearn. This is a valley through which his railway ran, linking Stirling to Perth. Enchanted by the area, it occurred to him that if a really luxurious hotel and golf resort were developed here, the Caledonian could rival the success of its competitors. Indeed, it might well siphon off custom from the Highland Railway at Royal Dornoch, the Great North of Scotland Railway at Cruden Bay, and the Glasgow & South Western Railway at Turnberry.

Matheson was an engineer by background and not an hotelier and having submitted plans to his Board in the autumn of 1912 he thought it sensible to find partners. A year later the go-ahead was given to back an enterprise calling itself Gleneagles Ltd. The Caledonian agreed to subscribe up to £25,000 but, as the project was being promoted by a private company, parliamentary authority had to be obtained. The wheels were set in motion and this was duly received under the Caledonian Railway Order Confirmation Act of 1913. With his groundwork complete, Matheson was now intent on action. Aiming to have the hotel up and running within fifteen months, by Easter 1915, he set about establishing the golf course first.

Immediately after Christmas and before the Scots made merry over New Year, he arranged for James Braid and Captain Cecil Hutchison to pay a visit. The idea was that Braid would design the course and Hutchison supervise the construction. Carters Seeds were on hand to prepare the topsoil. Their remit was to produce an inland course as fine or finer than any other in the land. All three liked what they saw for, quite apart from the views, the terrain was of resilient moorland turf on a gravel sub-soil and quick to drain. So they set to work with a will.

Soon bills had to be met. Fees for Braid and Hutchison were modest enough at £120 plus their expenses; but Carters charges topped £12,500. And that was just the beginning for the overall plans were as ambitious as they were comprehensive. They included an electric power station, a laundry, central-heating plant, a garage, gate lodges and a clubhouse. All were ancillary to the hotel which was the main investment.

Knowing only too well the need to attract customers to this major undertaking, the Caledonian discussed with the North British Railways the introduction of special fares for golfers. Within a month this was agreed and the concept sensibly broadened to include all the golf course stations served from Glasgow.

Then came the Great War. In December 1914, with Gleneagles Ltd suffering from a cashflow crisis, the Caledonian authorised more than £50,000 to discharge their liabilities. Though work on the hotel ceased, construction of the golf course went ahead as usual. However, when the local Territorial Army unit was to request its use as a rifle range, the Caledonian refused point blank, arguing that Braid's design was inviolate and the Army should reconsider their proposals from scratch.

By 1918 the hotel was still a shell. However, the course was playable and the following May it opened. It was then the railway company had cold feet, fearing the incomplete hotel might become a white elephant. So when an inquiry was received from the USA about buying it along with the course, the directors breathed a sigh of relief. Their aim now was to extricate themselves and to break even; provided they were reimbursed, they agreed to complete the hotel. As it was the offer lapsed. That meant there was then no option for the Caledonian other than put on a brave face, take Gleneagles Ltd under its wing completely and promote golf over the course they christened the 'King's'.

In 1920 they put up £150 in prize money for a tournament organised by Donald Matheson. The hotel was now his responsibility and his colleagues were distancing themselves from it. That May Gleneagles hosted its first championship, but Matheson had been astute, performed a neat sidestep and devolved the main responsibility upon the North British Rubber Company. Among other things they manufactured golf balls, well-favoured by golfers and bearing a distinctive livery of diagonal red dimples.

Several more tournaments were organised; the Scottish Professional Championship; the Four Day £650 Glasgow *Herald* Knockout Tournament; a 36-hole amateur event which followed on immediately; and the Scottish

Amateur Championship which was sponsored by the Dundee *Evening Telegraph and Post.*

All the while, Matheson as General Manager was expected to cope with the accommodation, arrange the catering and not to neglect his railway. His job was on the line but Gleneagles was his concept and, determined to see it through, he rose to the challenge ably. Little in stature if big in mind, he laid on special flights to the course from Glasgow's airport at Renfrew.

It was in that first Glasgow *Herald* tournament that Scotsman George Duncan showed the world how Gleneagles should be played. In the final he defeated Arnaud Massy by 3/2 and in so doing he won the first prize of £160. That was the largest purse seen to date in professional golf. Three days of delightful weather had given way to rolling mist. There were no distant glens to charm, a dull light had replaced the earlier dazzle and moisture lay heavily on the greens. Conditions favoured target golf and the bold putter. In front of thousands of spectators to include the defeated professionals who stayed on to watch, Duncan was relentless. Out in 36 he stood 5 up. Then on the tenth, trying a clean flick from the sand, he failed and only escaped from the trap with his fourth shot. The pace slackened but a grand run up at the fourteenth, Denty

King's Course, Gleneagles *(courtesy of Gleneagles Golf Club)*

Den, earned him a winning 3. In a moment he was dormie. Perfect halves were to follow and that was that.

At the prize-giving J. H. Taylor offered the vote of thanks. All had admired the diabolical cunning of the cavernous bunkers. Were they now to receive the anathema of the golfing public, which he thought they might, that would only go to prove their efficiency and the cunning of Braid's strategy. And as a Scotsman had won, he was sure this would be an inspiration to thousands. Equally prophetic as J. H. was the *Herald's* golf correspondent on writing,

> Success such as this should inspire Duncan with confidence in his ability to gain the greatest honour of all that has until now been denied him. The Open Championship at Deal a few weeks hence would give him the opportunity of retrieving his previous failures. After Gleneagles he need fear no one – except himself.

Indeed, Duncan was to be inspired. Trailing early on, he succeeded in winning the Open at Deal with two incredible last rounds of 71 and 72.

After such a year of frenetic activity, with completion of the hotel still nowhere in sight, Matheson was determined that at the very least there should be no let up where golf was concerned. In May 1921 the Scottish Professional Championship was held again. Next month in a masterly public relations coup, and as a prelude to the Glasgow *Herald* tournament, came a ten-a-side international match between Great Britain and the USA. The first of its kind, it was a forerunner of the Ryder Cup which followed six years later. With foursomes in the morning, and singles in the afternoon, the home team won by 9 matches to 3 with three halved.

This was a triumph, though in hindsight it marked the end of an era. For many of the British team it was virtually their swansong. Only Arthur Havers was under 30. Taylor was 50, Braid and Vardon were each a year older. With an average age of 41, some were to conclude that our younger men do not come on as quickly as they do in America. The sad fact is that the British were never again to dominate at the highest level. In the next 60 years of the Open Championship only ten winners were British, and three of these wins were taken by Henry Cotton! So the occasion was one to cherish and be remembered.

First out in the foursomes, George Duncan and his good friend 34-year-old Abe Mitchell, took on Jock Hutchison and Walter ('the Haig') Hagen. The Americans were outdriven but they made up for this by superior putting. The truth is in that department the home side left a lot to be desired. On the first green Mitchell missed from a yard and two holes later Duncan putted up short. The wily Hagen took advantage and laid a stymie. Winning the next hole, the

Americans went 2 up. But the Britons clawed back. Then they slipped to allow the Americans to be 2 up with 5 to go. But as most golfers know, this all too seldom wins.

Mitchell drove the green at Denty Den, the short par 4, then rammed in a stout putt after Duncan had been woefully timid. The next hole was halved. Then Hagen collared a saving putt of a good ten feet at the short sixteenth. With Mitchell's pitch to the seventeenth stopping only a yard from the hole to go level, the gallery sensed the tide was on the turn.

Then, to horrified gasps, Mitchell whipped his drive to the left at the last. Ever opportune, Hagen followed with a beauty. Now the odds against defeat swung violently to something like 100 to one. Duncan had to hack out sideways. Seconds later Hutchison was nicely on the green in two. Mitchell looked stern before rallying to play a fine pitch from the edge of the eighteenth green on the Queen's course. It finished within eight yards of the hole. Hagen overputted. Again Duncan's effort appeared gentle. However the ball ran and ran till it trickled in. All of a sudden Hutchison was staring at a five-footer and it was he who was struggling. But he kept wonderfully still and down it went for a half to relief all round.

Behind them Vardon and Ray opened with a birdie and were 3 up after 3. They trounced their men by 5/4. Close on their heels the formidable pairing of Braid and Taylor were out in 35 to be 2 up. Then their long game became ragged but excellent putting saved them. On the thirteenth and fourteenth greens first one and then other contributed an eight-yarder. At the sixteenth Taylor holed from ten foot and, finally, they stood on the last tee dormie. Here Braid pushed his brassie and a safe 4 by Clarence Hackney and Fred McLeod earned the Americans a half. With Havers and Jack Ockenden turning in 34 to win comfortably, and Jack Sherlock and Taylor squeaking home on the last in a scrappy affair, the British had a lead of 3 points to nil.

After lunch, Duncan, as the Open Champion and course specialist, led out the singles against U.S. Professional Champion Jock Hutchison. They played at such speed those watching were reported as coming in 'with faces very hot and very red'. In less than two hours they were treated to a marathon and a faultless game. Though Duncan was to miss three very holeable putts, he stood on the fourteenth tee 4 up. When he duly won by 2/1 he had played just 68 shots.

No one would normally accuse Mitchell and Hagen of slow play but they were quite three holes behind. What a dogfight this was, with never more than a hole in it. Early on Mitchell looked the more impressive, but Hagen kept on sinking very awkward putts to turn one up. At the thirteenth Mitchell squared and once more drove Denty Den to regain a lead he had not held since the fourth.

He nearly won the fifteenth, but a 30-yard putt slipped past the hole by two inches, and the Haig got down a nasty one to halve. At Wee Bogle Mitchell was bunkered left and Hagen struck a classy tee shot which bit and bounced back. Now level, Mitchell belted a raker with his driver. But it availed little. Hagen's first putt stormed six yards past and his second set a stymie to give rather a sad half in 5. At the last Hagen again took three putts and Mitchell, right of the green in two, was let off the hook with a half. Perhaps justly!

The pipe-smoking Ted Ray was always struggling against the American captain Emmett French and duly lost by 2/1. But Taylor, after starting with a horrid 6, soon looked well in command against Fred McLeod. Once more the critical hole was Denty Den. Both drives were bunkered left of the green. McLeod cleverly used the slope behind the hole for the ball struck the green high up and, to appreciative applause, came crawling back to within one foot. Taylor tried to follow suit but his ball scuttled over the bank down the other side and he called out, 'That's enough, Fred'. Shortly his position of 3 up and 5 to go was down to 2 up with 3 to go. Then the unthinkable occurred. Taylor three-putted Wee Bogle, hooked at the seventeenth, and took another three putts at the last to lose all three and the match. The tough man had beaten himself!

If the Americans were poised for a counter attack, they reckoned without Harry Vardon. He was enjoying himself hugely. As in the morning, he was back to his very best. Out in 34 with three birdies, he had driven beautifully with that easy effortless swing. His irons were timed straight and true, and on the greens he was confidence himself. Tom Kerrigan did well to stick with him for 17 holes, since one more 4 would have earned Vardon a round of 68.

Braid was in convincing form with birdies at the first and fifth. Even with 5 at the ninth he was out in 35 and 5 up, well on his way to defeating Clarence Hackney by 5/4. Meanwhile, after turning 3 up Arthur Havers weakened in the second nine to lose 2/1, but Ockenden was trampling on McLean 6/5. Sherlock' steadiness and tidy putting saw him untroubled and Josh Taylor fought like a tiger. One down at the turn, he won three holes in a row from the twelfth, and though he lost a ball at the fifteenth in the morass on the left, he finished off Bill Mehlhorn with a 2 at Wee Bogle. Mehlhorn's style was compared to a hod carrier but he was not to be trifled with. He was good enough to be tied in the lead with Bobby Jones after 36 holes in the 1926 Open, and he played top for the U.S. in the very first Ryder Cup match the next year.

Overall the day's play resulted in a resounding victory, and had Taylor at 50 quite uncharacteristically not weakened in the closing stages, the result would have been 10 matches to 2. In the aftermath the Glasgow *Herald* wrote up Gleneagles as 'perhaps the finest inland course in the world' – adulation exceeding even the brief set by Donald Matheson to James Braid and Cecil Hutchison. To mark the occasion the Duchess of Atholl presented a medal to each participant.

The result proved a fillip to the British that week. Abe Mitchell went on to win the big tournament. The format for this was unusual for after 27 holes of stroke play, 16 qualified for a match-play knockout. In the final Joe Kirkwood succumbed by 7/6.

With the golf course settling in to such acclaim, there was progress of all sorts behind the scenes. Gleneagles station had been reconstructed at a cost of more than £5,000 and now assumed certain architectural features in common with those planned for the hotel. Having commissioned the new work, Gleneagles Ltd considered the expense should be met by the Caledonian. They agreed. The clubhouse was in the throes of being extended, and Donald Matheson won further confidence when he was authorised to purchase additional land for a second course to be known as the 'Queen's'.

Winning new custom was the name of the game. In pursuance of this, in August a novel fares scheme was introduced aimed specifically at golfers. On Saturdays a day-return ticket to a station serving a golf course was to cost the same as a single, provided it was purchased before midday. Other developments included plans for a professional's shop, caddies' quarters, and houses for the

Queen's Course, Gleneagles *(courtesy of Gleneagles Golf Club)*

professional and the green staff. Also, to create an impression on visitors arriving by train, a new, 25-foot-wide road was constructed from the station to the golf course.

By February 1923 the railway company had become the sole shareholder in Gleneagles Ltd. To extend its powers and enable it to take over the land and maintain the course, an act of Parliament was required. That spring, under Matheson's prodding, 500 men were working on the hotel. To pacify any doubters he was able to report to the Board that more than 20,000 lunches and 21,000 teas had been served in the clubhouse. Moreover, accommodation with the County Council, who had earlier opposed closure of certain rights of way, had been reached. In all the auguries were now promising.

June was busy. The popular Glasgow *Herald* tournament was won by Arthur Havers. Like Duncan two years earlier, he went on to win the Open, this time at Troon. Good courses produce good winners and Gleneagles very much fitted this mould as it calls for skill in handling sloping lies and coping with large undulating greens – features commonly found on the great seaside links. Other tournaments to be hosted by Gleneagles included the Scottish Universities and the Scottish Police. Then the Blackface Sheepbreeders Association chose it for their annual jamboree. Either by accident or by design, very different spheres of influence were being cultivated.

That July under the regrouping of Britain's railways into four companies, the Caledonian became part of the London Midland & Scottish Railway. Matheson came out of it well as Deputy General Manager of the Scottish section; his involvement with Gleneagles had won him kudos after all.

Finally, Matheson's dream was to come true. On Saturday 7 June 1924 the hotel opened just in time for the Glasgow *Herald* tournament the following week. That was won once again by course specialist George Duncan. At 12s 6d for a single room and double that for an en-suite bathroom, the hotel charges were not unkindly. Inclusive terms started at £1 10s a day. Green fees were modest – just 2s 6d a day or 12s 6d for the week – and at last Sunday play was permitted.

Marketing of the hotel was as masterly as of the golf course and national attention was gained. On that opening night the orchestra under Henry Hall was broadcast live. Something of a technical revolution was accomplished when the sound was relayed by a land line to a transmitter in Glasgow. While dancers, svelte and sophisticated in evening dress, glided and twirled, hotel guests were astonished to hear the ballroom music pouring forth from the radio in their bedrooms. Thereafter Henry Hall's dance music was broadcast twice weekly. He proved such a success he was to set up 32 orchestras for railway hotels before moving on to the coveted position of Dance Orchestra leader with the BBC, but at half his previous comfortable salary!

Matheson saw that nothing was left to chance. Promotion of the golf course and hotel continued assiduously. In September 1924 a 72-hole exhibition match was arranged. George Duncan was a natural choice to represent Scotland against Scots born American Macdonald Smith. The prize was 100 guineas and a silver souvenir cup in the form of a pilgrim flask was presented by White Horse Distillers. The golf was to be sensational: play of that quality had never before been seen.

The Glasgow *Herald* covered it in detail and enthused. On the morning of the event the paper commented:

It is an interesting encounter, which Duncan ought at any rate to win. Both have been holidaying recently in Scotland, Duncan at North Berwick and Smith at his native town of Carnoustie, and both have been playing very well.

In knowledge of Gleneagles Duncan will start with a great advantage and a great inspiration. Some of the best golf he has ever played has been at Gleneagles. He won .. 'The Glasgow *Herald* Thousand Guineas Tournament .. again this year by the most amazing golf that even he has ever played beating Abe Mitchell over the 36 holes final by 8/7, and playing 29 holes of such a testing course in seven stokes under 4s. Gleneagles then should inspire Duncan to play his best this week. Smith, on the other hand, played his first round over the course last month .. and went round .. in approximately 67.

So the scene was set. The *Herald* added for good measure,

Special travelling facilities are being given in connection with the match by the London Midland & Scottish Railway Company, through whose courtesy the match is being played at Gleneagles.

Next day's paper merely recorded that the match stood at an interesting halfway situation. It would seem that the autumn diary and forthcoming events such as the Boys Championship, the Walker Cup, and expectations held of Joyce and Roger Wethered, were more newsworthy.

By Wednesday 3 September matters were quite different. There were no less than four headlines,

SMITH WINS
DUNCAN'S FAILURE AT GLENEAGLES
LEAD LOST AND REGAINED
SENSATIONAL PLAY

The report began:

Macdonald Smith, the Scoto-American, beat George Duncan here this afternoon by 4 and 3 after a prolonged fight over two days. That is a bald result of a day of as interesting, at time as dazzling, golf as even Gleneagles has ever seen.

The second two rounds were played on a sweltering day before a gallery of 3,000. Duncan had started the morning 3 down. The previous day's leisurely atmosphere was replaced by the tense expectation that every stroke mattered – as indeed it did. Duncan turned the score on its head. Out in 32 in the morning he climbed to 2 up. It was then Macdonald Smith's turn for fireworks. He roared home in 32. Yet this could have been the ridiculous score of 29 since on three greens out of four he was stymied; and only a brilliant 3 by Duncan at the last, who struck a long iron a yard from the pin, prevented the American from lunching 2 up.

In the afternoon, before a spellbound gallery, Duncan started where he left off. Following an enormous drive of quite 300 yards, he slotted a two-yard putt for a birdie to draw level. Smith was saved at the next: his ball rebounded off a spectator on to the green instead of flying into a bunker at the back. All square after 5 holes, it was then that,

> Duncan missed chance after chance to win or halve the holes. It was this disastrous patch that lost Duncan a match he looked like winning. He did not play the putts carelessly, but he missed them – and every handicap man in the crowd would have backed himself to hole them.

Even then he was out in 35 but he turned 2 down instead of 2 up. He had missed twice from two yards, once from a yard at the short eighth after Macdonald Smith had failed to pitch yet another stymie, and then again from four feet at the ninth. That was four shots lost.

Soon 3 down, Duncan birdied the twelfth, but Smith came back at him with a brilliant 3 at Braid's Brawest. He hit a devastating long iron into this rolling 450-yard hole and, with the green sloping awkwardly away, calmly sunk the putt. He was now 3 up and, when Duncan's ball hung on the lip of the cup at the fifteenth, Smith faced an easy putt after the most skilful of pitches from the rough. He popped it in for the hole and the match by 4 and 3.

Goodness only knows what the score would have been without stymies, but Macdonald Smith had followed up his morning 69 by being four under 4s with a short hole still to come and Duncan, himself four under 4s on the day, was vanquished. On shaking hands, Smith was immediately surrounded by admirers who escorted him back to the clubhouse. His brilliance had captivated, and the fair-minded Scottish crowd which had been largely on

Gleneagles poster – dramatic, if perhaps inaccurate *(courtesy of the National Railway Museum/Science & Society Picture Library)*

Duncan's side cheered unreservedly, recognising that on the day the better man had won.

Twelve months later in September 1925 the Queen's course was opened. Picturesque and less taxing than the King's, it offered exclusive seclusion. Matheson's concept was substantially complete. Gleneagles, formerly Glendevon before the golf course was built, and earlier still Glen d'eglise, was a choice name to conjure with. While there is a little church in the glen dedicated to the local Haldane family, apparently there never were any eagles!

Three years later, resentful at 'being mixed up with a modern railway hotel' a scion was to complain how the name Gleneagles had been purloined. He claimed his family had owned it since the twelfth century. Quite apart from the sustained publicity, and the fact that every single item of hotel cutlery had Gleneagles stamped upon it, he was too late to bring about any change. In practice, the Caledonian had not been as cavalier as he thought. On seeking to change the name of the station from Crieff Junction to Gleneagles – for a branch line ran from there to the Highland resort of Crieff – they did have discussions in 1911 with the head of the family, Lord Camperdown. He was impressed by the prestige of the project and agreed. It was just that the request had not formally embraced the hotel. That was taken for granted.

As it was the reputation of Gleneagles was soaring. The hotel advertised itself as 'The Eighth Wonder' and 'Nonesuch in Europe'. The press outdid each other in extravagance hailing it as 'New Palace among the Scottish mountains', 'The Switzerland of Scotland', and 'The Playground of the Gods'; and rather dramatically, if inaccurately, the golf course was promoted with a giant eagle astride a mountain crag.

Other railway companies were extolling golf with the aim of encouraging rail travel and the LMS was to join in. With the hotel now open, they published their book Golf at its Best on the LMS. Purple prose explained how nature had smiled graciously and sweetly, that on a clear day the view from the bedroom window stretched to 70 miles of grand Highland country featuring great sweeps of mysterious moor, huge splashes of maroon heather, stains of olive green furzes, and exquisite blue/grey mountains. Today all remains as it was, truly a 'pageantry of panoramic loveliness' in enchanted ground; though the claim that one would feel ten years younger after a visit is perhaps harder to countenance!

Certainly, once at the hotel, there was no need to leave, other than maybe to shoot. Apart from golf, there was private fishing, nine hard tennis courts, a swimming pool and a superb croquet lawn. Indoors there was a hairdressing salon, a post office, a bank and two ballrooms. A hotel bus met those arriving by train while the hotel garage was large enough for 80 limousines. Chauffeurs had their own special block – a far cry from servants accommodation under the eaves in poky rooms offered by some railway hotels 40 years earlier.

As with the Cruden Bay Hotel of the GNOSR, Gleneagles was able to make use of more than the obvious railway facilities and its construction was aided by stone carried from a disused railway viaduct via a private siding. Matheson never missed a trick! After the Great War and until the hotel opened its door, Pullman cars would make use of the disused siding. Indeed, at the outset railway carriages served as the professional's shop and the clubhouse, allowing golfers to enjoy breakfast a stone's-throw from the first tee.

Later the Gleneagles Puffer, as the little shunting locomotive was called, ran to the kitchen door conveying essential requirements. These included coal, dry goods, linen from the railway's laundry at Edinburgh, and wine from the famed LMS cellars below the St Pancras hotel in London. Under internal accounting procedures this goods system lingered on until the Beeching era of the 1960s.

From the outset the hotel's clientele was distinctly upper crust. Many were wealthy Americans of Scottish extraction. To attract ongoing attention among the elite of amateur golf, and to launch the new Queen's course, the LMS commissioned a handsome silver quaich from silversmiths in Glasgow. The Glasgow *Herald* duly did it justice with a fine photograph, and this became the prize for the Silver Tassie, taking over from the amateur event that used to follow on immediately after the professional tournament.

The inaugural winner in September 1925 was top British golfer Cyril Tolley. He had the highly respectable scores of 71 on the King's and 70 on the Queen's. Wealthy golfing socialites were now to leap at the chance to compete, and to stay in what all seemed to agree was the outstanding country hotel in Britain.

One winner who drank a toast from the quaich in 1929, was Rex Hartley. A director of the well-known Hartley's jam business, he enjoyed the friendship of the Prince of Wales. At Cambridge he had been captain of golf but his Lancia was frequently seen outside London's Kit Kat club and this passion for night-life and dancing caused him to be rusticated. His opposite number at Oxford, Raymond Oppenheimer, suffered the same fate. As neither university wished to be deprived of their talents, it was quietly agreed both would play in the varsity

Upper crust: the LMS flagship the *Silver Jubilee*, bound for Glasgow from London Euston
(courtesy of Locomotive and General Railways Photographs)

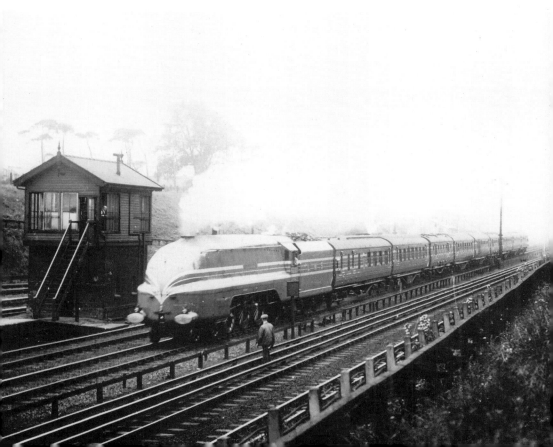

match although not against each other. Rex was a marvel at chipping and putting and duly won his foursome and his single.

Many clubs were to know Rex Hartley as a member. At Gleneagles he had entered from Sunningdale. His brother Lister was an adept performer and not to be outdone. He matched Rex's Silver Tassie victory in the following year and again in 1932. But each time he chose to enter from Chislehurst where he learned his game. No two brothers since have ever equalled their golfing eminence in amateur circles. Both played in the home internationals and in the Walker Cup; both won the St George's Grand Challenge Cup. Rex twice won the *Golf Illustrated* Gold Vase, then equalled Lister's two victories when he captured the Silver Tassie again in 1938.

They were heady days and Rex's life seemed charmed. Record holder at Chislehurst with a 63, when he had eight 3s in nine holes from the fifth to the thirteenth, he had featured on a Churchman's cigarette card drawn by Mel the cartoonist. Perhaps appearances flattered. In 1942, aged only 36, he died from an infection caused by injuries on falling out of a window six months earlier. Fates were unkind to Lister too. Ever gentle, he succumbed years later to Parkinson's disease.

During the Second World War, the hotel was requisitioned as a convalescent

Gleneagles Hotel *(courtesy of Gleneagles Golf Club)*

hospital. Afterwards it was never quite the same, for the glamour attached to that social era typified by those Hartley brothers was all but at an end. Money was tight, and although the rich sought out Gleneagles, few could vie with the resources of the Honourable Mrs Muriel Gamage. Daughter of Lord Hirst, who was known as 'The Father of the GEC' (General Electric Company), her husband Leslie became Joint Managing Director and was himself Chairman. For many years the two spent August at Gleneagles and she became an institution. Her passion for flowers was legendary and other suites were denuded of occasional tables to display them and to permit her gin and tonic to fall easily to hand!

Sadly the lure of Silver Tassie diminished since a few days in Gleneagles was to prove too costly for most would-be competitors. The English never again dominated, while the Scots tended to steer clear of the hotel and opt for bed-and-breakfast accommodation in Auchterarder or Perth. As a result the tournament was reduced to just another local event and so quietly died.

To keep Gleneagles to the fore a Professional/Amateur foursomes tournament was sponsored by the Saxone shoe company. It attracted the big names from Britain, though not from abroad. When Saxone withdrew, the hotel took up the sponsorship itself. It was good fun but not a vital part of the more serious merry-go-round of professional golf. Less and less were the major names inclined to participate.

In 1981 when Government decided the railway industry should stick to railways, and no doubt mindful that sooner or later state control might cease, the hotel was sold along with all the others in the British Transport Hotels group. Private ownership brought new investment. Much more than when it was tagged as 'Britain's Premier Sports Hotel', the appeal was now of a complete resort. That is how it has continued and why it continues to delights the rich, the famous, and personalities from the world of showbusiness. Today very few would wish to quarrel with the sentiments of that LMS publication of 1925 when Del Leigh lauded Gleneagles as,

> the most wonderful sporting holiday place I have ever visited – and ever wish to visit.

Aside from the sad desolation that has long permeated the railway station, Gleneagles is still special. Here most emphatically is enchanted ground, for which all credit to that railway engineer, visionary, and man of action, Donald Matheson. Gleneagles was the last of the great railway enterprises devoted to golf. Yet it is timeless and a fitting memorial to the era when, in the minds of Britain's leading families, Scotland was for holidays. That is a truth now being learned by others the world over.

Bibliography

Adams, John, *The Parks of Musselburgh* (Grant)

Aldeburgh Golf Club, The First Hundred Years

Alliss, Peter, *The Opens* (Collins)

Baddiel, Sarah, *Golf – The Golden Years* (Bracken Books)

Baird, Archie, *Golf on Gullane Hill*

Bartlett, Michael, *The Golf Book* (Arbor House)

Braid, James, *Advanced Golf*

The British Railway Journal, Summer 1955

Carter, Oliver, *An Illustrated History of British Railways Hotels, 1838–1983* (Silver Link Publishing)

Cole, Beverley, *Golf and Railway Advertising* (Friend of NRM Journal)

Coleridge, J. K., *Sheringham Golf Club Centenary Year*

Cossey, Rosalind, *Ladies in Golf* (Orbis)

Cousins, Geoffrey, *Golf in Britain* (Routledge Kegan & Paul)

Darwin, Bernard, *Every Idle Dream* (Collins)

Darwin, Bernard, *Golf* (Burke)

Darwin, Bernard, *Mostly Golf (Selections by Peter Ryde)*, (Black)

Bernard Darwin, *Pack Clouds Away* (Collins)

Dryden, W. A. S., *Panmure Golf Club* (Panmure GC)

Ellis, Hamilton, *Railway Art* (Ashe & Grant)

Emblem, Tommy, *Around New Zealand* (T Emblem)

Farnie, H. B., *The Golfer's Manual, 1857* (reprint, Dropmore Press)

Farr, A. D., *The Campbeltown & Machrihanish Light Railway* (Oakwood Press)

Forres Club History

Golfing Trifles (Michael Joseph)

Goodban, John, *The Royal North Devon Golf Club, 1864–1964*

Goodner, Ross, *Golf's Greatest*

Hackney, Stewart, *Carnoustie Links: Courses and Players*

Hagen, Walter, *The Walter Hagen Story* (Heinemann)

Hajducki, Andrew, *North Berwick & Gullane Branch Lines* (Oakwood Press)

Hamer, Malcolm, *The Ryder Cup – The Players* (Kingswood)

Jones, Ernest, *Swinging into Golf* (Nicholson & Watson)

Joseph, Michael, *Happy Holidays – The Golden Age of Railway Posters* (Pavilion)

Joy, David, *Regional Railway – History of the Railway*, GB Vol. 14

Lewis, Peter, *Golfiana*, Vol. 6, No. 1, 1994

Lindsay, Stewart, *The Nairn Golf Club, 1887–1987*

Leigh, Del, *Golf at its Best on the LMS* (LMS)

Leigh-Bennett, E. P., *Some Friendly Fairways* (Southern Railway)

McConachie, John Andrew, *The Moray Golf Club at Lossiemouth* (Moray GC)

McDiarmid, D. J. *100 Years of Machrihanish, 1876–1976*

McKinlay, Sam, *Scottish Golf and Golfers* (George Outram/Ailsa)

Macgregor, Ian, *Tain Golf Club, 1890–1990*

Mackay, F., *A. J. Balfour: Intellectual Statesman* (Ruddock)

Mackie, Keith, *Open Championship Golf Courses of Britain* (Aurum Press)

Macmillan, Nigel, *The Campbeltown–Machrihanish Light Railway* (David & Charles)

Mitchell, Joseph, *Reminiscences of My Life in the Highlands*, Vol. 1 (David & Charles)

Mitchell, Joseph, *Reminiscences of My Life in the Highlands*, Vol. 2 (David & Charles)

Mitchell, M. J., *Cruden Bay Hotel Tramway* (Tramway Review No. 122)

Mitchell, W. M., *Chislehurst Golf Club* (Grant & Hobbs)

Moreton, John F., *The Golf Courses of James Braid* (Grant Books)

Morrison, Alex, *The Impossible Art of Golf Writing* (Oxford University Press)

The North British Railway Golfers and Anglers Guide, 1921

Prain, Eric, *The Oxford and Cambridge Golfing Society* (Eyre & Spottiswoode)

Prebble, John, *The High Girders* (Martin Secker & Warburg)

Richards, Jeffrey, and John Mackenzie, *The Railway Station – A Social History* (Oxford University Press)

Ridley, Jane, and Claire Percy, *The Letters of Arthur Balfour and Lady Elcho*

(Hamish Hamilton)

Royal Dornoch, *Club History*

Sampson, Curt, *Hogan* (Rutledge Hill)

Scotland for the Holidays: The Central Highlands (LMS)

Simpson, Eric, *Discovering Banff, Moray and Nairn* (John Donald)

Smail, David Cameron, *Prestwick Golf Club, Birth Place of the Open* (Prestwick GC)

Steel, Donald, *The Golfers Bedside Book* (Batsford)

Strathpeffer Golf Club, A Hundred Years (Strathpeffer GC)

Taylor, Derek, and David Bush, *The Golden Age of British Hotels* (Northwood)

Thomas, John, *Forgotten Railways – North East Scotland* (David & Charles)

Thomas, John, *The Skye Railway* (David St John Thomas)

Tiltman, H. Hessell, *James Ramsay Macdonald – Labour's Man of Destiny* (Jarrolds)

Turner, Barry, *The Dornoch Light Railway* (Dornoch Press)

Wellborn, Nigel, *Lost Lines Scotland* (Ian Allan)

Western Gailes: A Club History

Index